DATE DUE

DEMCO 38-296

The Marshall Cavendish Illustrated History of

POPULAR MUSIC

Volume 11
1970-1971

MARSHALL CAVENDISH
NEW YORK, LONDON, TORONTO, SYDNEY

Reference Edition Published 1990

ion

a. Vicenza.

Reference edition produced by DPM Services.

© Orbis Publishing Ltd.MCMLXXXIX
© Marshall Cavendish Ltd.MCMLXXXIX

Set ISBN 1-85436-015-3

Library of Congress Cataloging in Publication Data

The Marshall Cavendish history of popular music.
        p.   cm.
    Includes index.
    ISBN 1-85435-026-9 (vol. 11)
    1. Popular music — History and criticism. 2. Rock music — History
and Criticism. I. Marshall Cavendish Corporation. II. Title:
History of popular music.
ML 3470. M36 1988
784. 5' 009 — dc19   88-21076
                                                                CIP
                                                                MN

Editorial Staff

Editor	Ashley Brown
Executive Editors	Adrian Gilbert
	Michael Heatley
Consultant Editors	Richard Williams
	Peter Brookesmith
Editorial Director	Brian Innes

Reference Edition Staff

Reference Editor	Mark Dartford
Revision Editor	Fran Jones
Consultant Editor	Michael Heatley
Art Editor	Graham Beehag

CONTENTS

CONTRIBUTORS

CLIVE ANDERSON

Co-author of *The Soul Book* and contributor to *Encyclopedia of Rock,* he has also written for *Black Music, Black Echoes, New Kommotion* and other magazines.

STEPHEN BARNARD

Has contributed to *Atlantic Rock, Melody Maker* and the *Rock Files* series. He also lectures at the City University, London.

DICK BRADLEY

Completed his PhD thesis on *British Popular Music in the Fifties* at the Centre of Contemporary Cultural Studies in Birmingham, England, and has also written articles for *Media, Culture & Society.*

JOHN BROVEN

Author of *Walking to New Orleans* and *South of Louisiana,* he has also contributed to *Nothing but the Blues* and *Encyclopedia of Rock.* He writes for *Blues Unlimited* and has also compiled several New Orleans rhythm and blues anthologies

ROB FINNIS

Author of *The Phil Spector Story* and *The Gene Vincent Story,* he has contributed to the major rock journals and runs a specialist record shop.

SIMON FRITH

A lecturer at the University of Warwick, England, he has built up a reputation over the last 15 years as one of the leading international commentators on rock music. He has co-edited the *Rock File* series, and written *The Sociology of Rock.*

PETER GURALNIK

Author of *Feel Like Going Home, Lost Highway* and *Nighthawk Blues,* his articles on blues, country and rock have appeared in *Rolling Stone,* the *Village Voice, Country Music, Living Blues,* the *New York Times* and the *Boston Phoenix.*

BILL HARRY

Founder member of UK's *Mersey Beat,* he later became news editor of *Record Mirror* and music columnist for *Weekend.* He is currently an independent PR for such artists as Suzi Quatro and Kim Wilde.

MARTIN HAWKINS

An acknowledged expert on the Sun era of rock'n'roll (author of *The Sun Story*), he writes for *Melody Maker, Time Barrier Express* and *Country Music*

BRIAN HOGG

Publisher of *Bam Balam,* which concentrates on US and UK bands of the Sixties, he has also written for such magazines as *New York Rocker* and *Record Collector.*

PETER JONES

Was editor of UK's *Record Mirror* from 1961 to 1969. He then became UK News editor of *Billboard* in 1977 and later UK and European Editor.

ROBIN KATZ

After 10 years in the Motown Press Office, she now writes freelance for *New Sound, New Styles, International Musician* and *Smash Hits.*

JOE McEWEN

An acknowledged authority on soul music, he has written for *Rolling Stone, Phonograph Record, Black Music,* the *Boston Phoenix* and Boston's *Real Paper.*

BILL MILLAR

As a freelance journalist he writes for *Melody Maker* and other rock papers. He is the author of *The Drifters* and *The Coasters.*

DAVID MORSE

Author of *Motown,* he lectures at the School of English and American Studies at Sussex University, England.

TONY RUSSELL

Editor of *Old Time Music* from 1971, he contributes regularly to *Blues Unlimited* and *Jazz Journal* and is the author of *Blacks, Whites and Blues.*

ROBERT SHELTON

Has written about blues, country and folk for the *New York Times,* London *Times, Listener, Time Out* and *Melody Maker.*

NICK TOSCHES

Author of *Hellfire,* a biography of Jerry Lee Lewis, he also writes for *New York Times* and *Village Voice.*

MICHAEL WATTS

Writes on popular arts for *The Los Angeles Times* and London *Times* and is rock columnist for *Records and Recording Magazine.*

ADAM WHITE

Has written about Motown for *Music Week* and *Black Echoes,* and scripted a six-hour documentary about the company and its music for US radio. Also worked as managing editor of *Billboard* magazine in New York.

Like A Rolling Stone

Bob Dylan's path through rock led from folk songs to gospel sounds

BOB DYLAN is rock's leading poet; he has one of its most distinctive voices; and the three major styles he used during the Sixties were enormously influential on the development of rock as a whole. More than this, he is also one of the most complex personalities in rock music, a man whose motives and intentions are shrouded and whose personal relationships are disturbing and hard to fathom.

There is no other lyricist in rock who remotely approaches the breadth of Dylan's achievement. In fact, his words are far more accurately described as poetry than lyrics. The seemingly effortless stream of puns and surreal images reminds one of the playing of the most inspired improvising musicians rather than of the normally banal and pedestrian words that make up the bulk of rock's lyrics. And whereas most of the words of a rock song usually have to be seen in the context of the music to have any power at all, Dylan's are quite capable of being examined at any level.

The sources of his poetry are clear – from French Symbolists of the late nineteenth century to the 'talking blues' of Woody Guthrie. It would be fairly accurate to say that he has done little that is truly original, from the point of view of form, and that much of his early impact was on people who had no knowledge of the originals (in the same way that his adoption of the e e cummings' method of typing without capital letters amused an audience who did not know the earlier poet's work). But what Dylan did was to borrow forms that he could then pour his own exciting, tumbling, inventive verbal talent into: rather like jazz musicians who borrowed musical forms to contain their improvisations – from dances like the quadrille to Broadway show tunes.

Inner visions

Such has been the impact of Dylan's poetry that it has tended to obscure the importance of his melodies. He has been the victim of more standard 'English literary criticism'-style analysis than any other rock songwriter. But although his tunes may not necessarily have the same depth as his lyrics, some have formed the basis of great rock songs. He could write 'hooks' that contain the essence of what the song is about as well as any Brill Building writer; he could write oblique, desperately sad melodies like 'The Gates Of Eden' and yet pump out the most raunchy confection in 'Rainy Day Women # 12 and 35'.

Then there is the voice – a whining, nasal drawl that would normally be considered ugly, but which is so distinctive, and which has such a unique way of articulating the lyrics that it has become one of the foundations of what we think of as rock vocals. This voice has been imitated all over the world – perhaps most flatteringly when another great rock singer,

Bob Dylan in 1965, the year he turned from acoustic folk to electric rock. Folk purists everywhere were outraged at Dylan's change of style – but it was a change that would prove fundamental in giving pop music a serious voice.

John Lennon, used its inflections in 1965 on his own highly Dylanesque composition, 'Norwegian Wood'.

With his voice and his verbal and musical gifts, Dylan could hardly be denied a great importance, but what gives him a central position in rock is his influence on the music's development. His early period as a folk artist proved the way for the singer-songwriter of a later era; his move to folk-rock in 1964-65 was crucial in bringing about the amalgam of styles that distanced 'rock' from 'pop' and gave it a new seriousness; while his decision to explore country roots in the late Sixties was again critical in finding fertile new directions for the music to develop.

Yet if Dylan's artistic contribution can be dissected, it is far harder to glimpse the man behind the achievement. His confusing and contradictory statements about himself; his almost pathological lying during his early years; the complication of his relationships with Suze Rotolo, Joan Baez and his wife Sara; his ambivalent attitude towards the political idealism that ostensibly inspired much of his early work; his convoluted attachment to drugs in the mid Sixties; and finally his conversion to 'Born Again' Christianity. None of these betoken a settled individual at ease with himself. But then could such an individual have produced the range of work that Dylan did?

ASHLEY BROWN

Dylan

The man and his music

THERE WAS a few minutes wait between sets as the band got into place. The compère seemed nervous, but the audience was in a good mood. Earlier in the day they had been dancing in the rain; now, the star that most of them had turned up to hear was about to appear on stage. Peter Yarrow, the MC, introduced him reverentially.

Yarrow, however, was not repaid in kind. The band crashed into the opening bars of a raucous, bluesy number. The folk-loving audience, slapped in the face by the din, were shocked, appalled, disgusted. They hadn't come to hear anything like *this*. The song, 'Maggie's Farm', summed it all up: 'Well I try my best/To be just like I am/But everybody wants you/To be just like them.' Thus hollered erstwhile folk hero Bob Dylan, who, on Sunday 25 July 1965, at the Newport Folk Festival, announced his conversion to the forces of rock'n'roll.

Rebel with a cause

It was neither the first nor the last conversion that Dylan was to announce, but musically it was the most significant. The development of rock in the Sixties and early Seventies was built on three revolutionary foundations: the Beatles, the Stones and Bob Dylan. And it was Dylan who, more than anyone else, showed that rock could be a form of art as well as entertainment. In 1965 it was not an idea that many people could easily assimilate – least of all the old guard at Newport who, like most adults, saw rock as trite, juvenile and, above all, nakedly commercial.

To Dylan himself there had never been any contradiction between seriousness and sales. Too much an original ever to write material that was not intelligent, Dylan had also had an irrepressible desire to be a rich and famous rock star since he was 15. Though he claimed later, at different times, that his 'first idol' had been Hank Williams or Woody Guthrie, his photograph in his high-school yearbook bears a rebellious legend stating his ambition: 'To join Little Richard.'

If folk music had been an obvious haven for Dylan's individualism, the declaration of allegiance to rock at Newport was no less natural, a return to the fold that had been his first love and inspiration. And it was perfectly in keeping with the questing and restless nature of his creativity, which has always – sometimes ruthlessly – sought its own satisfactions.

Dylan was always an outsider, even as a child. He was born Robert Allen Zimmerman in Duluth, Minnesota, on 24 May 1941, and moved with his family to Hibbing when he was six. His father Abraham kept an electrical goods store on Fifth Avenue, just off the main street. Young Robert Zimmerman fitted neither into his father's way of life – industry, thrift, nurture of the family business that he expected Robert to take over in due course – nor into the depressed, fiercely conven-

tional, overwhelmingly Catholic mining community. Music seems to have been second nature to him. He taught himself to play the piano at about the age of eight or nine, and the guitar – a mail-order model – at about 10. From his hours spent in Crippa's, the local record store, he discovered Hank Williams. And then he discovered black music, beamed out on late-night radio shows from Little Rock, Arkansas, and Chicago. But when he started his first band, the Golden Chords, the music proved a shade too hairy for its

Below: The young Robert Zimmerman as pictured in the Hibbing High School yearbook, 1959. Above: Folk singer Woody Guthrie, a prime influence on Dylan's early career. Opposite: Late-Sixties Dylan.

intended audience. He also took to roaring around on a Harley-Davidson motorcycle, his girlfriend Echo Star Helstrom hanging on the back. Occasionally his father would send him out to collect debts from his poorer customers, and it was probably then that he gained an insight into life on the other side of the tracks, and, particularly the reality of strikes, murder and struggle that made up the violent history of mining on the Mesabi Iron Range – subjects that he was later to describe with such insight in his songs.

Bobby Zimmerman could not get away from Hibbing fast enough, yet it is hard to imagine that his peculiar talents would have developed quite as richly as they did in any other community. His wayward character has always seemed to need something against which to rebel – and with which to identify at the same time. He found Hibbing stifled him – yet its philistine and conformist atmosphere forced him to develop his talent. 'The town that I grew up in is the one that has left me with my legacy visions' he wrote later.

Dylan in Dinkytown

Even in those early days, as plain Bobby Zimmerman, it was music that gave him his identity: just what kind of music would satisfy that ambition seems to have been immaterial. In July 1959 Zimmerman graduated from high school and in September enrolled at the University of Minnesota in Minneapolis. He made instantly for the coffeehouses of Dinkytown, the gathering place of 'ex-everythings . . . bums of all motivations, complexions and ages, and folkies'. His response to this new milieu was to conform to its nonconformity. He no longer spun yarns about playing piano with Little Richard, which would not have impressed that particular crowd, but invented stories about riding freight trains instead.

His behaviour suggests that his adoption of folk music at this time was in part a genuine identification with the idiom and in part sheer opportunism. Folk music presented him with a form and a style in which he could develop his talent; and there in Dinkytown was a ready-made audience. And he could scarcely have failed to notice that folk was rapidly gaining a substantial national following.

It was then that Bobby Zimmerman became Bob Dylan. Along with the new name he invented a new past: he claimed to be from Oklahoma, to have played piano with Bobby Vee, to have worked in carnivals, to have met some of the great blues singers on his travels.

His singing was, by all accounts, terrible at first; fired from the Ten O'Clock Scholar for driving away the customers, he resurfaced, undaunted, at the Purple Onion coffee house. He picked up songs wherever he could and, by mid 1960, had improved enough to be offered his first professional job – playing piano in a strip joint in Central City, Colorado.

It was in the autumn of that year that he discovered *Bound For Glory*, the autobiography of Woody Guthrie; before long he was saying that he had met his new hero years before, in California. But this was more than just another obsession, for Guthrie's example and songs gave Dylan the identity for which he was searching. Just before Christmas 1960 he left Minneapolis for New York, arriving there the following January. On his first night in the city he sang a couple of numbers at the Café Wha in Greenwich Village and within a couple of days had managed to meet

Woody Guthrie, then at Greystone Hospital in New Jersey. Through further meetings at a mutual friend's apartment a friendship and respect grew up between the dying singer and the young admirer.

Innocent children

Dylan soon found a niche for himself among the Greenwich Village folk singers, played Monday nights at Gerde's Folk City, gathered material from every possible source, and was actually billed at Gerde's in mid April for two weeks as supporting act to no less a legend than John Lee Hooker.

Dylan's peers in Greenwich Village – Dave Van Ronk, Bob Gleason, the Clancy Brothers and Ramblin' Jack Elliott among them – disregarded what they came to recognise as the singer's fantasies about his past because they saw that his was a genuine and original talent, rough at the edges though it still was. Said Van Ronk: 'Whatever he said off stage, on stage he told the truth as best he knew it.' By the summer he was well enough known to be asked to play harmonica on a new Harry Belafonte album. Overjoyed at the chance, he walked out on the session after only one track, 'Midnight Special', had been put in the can because he couldn't bear Belafonte's insistence on endless retakes.

Nonetheless, despite this somewhat unprofessional attitude, it was through session work – playing harmonica for Texan folkie Carolyn Hester – that he landed his recording contract with Columbia. Dylan was present when producer John Hammond visited Hester to discuss the album she was about to record. Dylan played, and Hammond was fascinated. Once the sessions were under way, Hammond was captivated and offered Dylan an unprecedented four per cent royalty on contract.

By this time Dylan was inseparable from Suze Rotolo, whom he had met in June 1961. Suze had an enormous, if not altogether witting effect on Dylan over the next three years or so. 'Two innocent children falling in love' was how one acquaintance described them in the beginning; but the idyll began to come apart in

Top right: Peter, Paul and Mary, Joan Baez, Dylan, the Freedom Singers and Pete Seeger at Newport, 1963. Top left: The same year, Bob sits by the pool strumming invisible guitar. Above: Dylan taps an acoustic foot. Below: With John Hammond.

November of the same year when Suze went to the studio with Dylan while he recorded his first album (total cost to Columbia: 402 dollars). She realised then and there that Dylan was going to be enormously successful – and the thought terrified her. He demanded total loyalty, resenting anything that distracted her attention from him. *Bob Dylan* was released in February 1962, and Suze was more than ever convinced that with Dylan she would have no life of her own.

The album was a superb and confident debut effort: only two of the songs are his own, 'Song To Woody' and 'Talkin' New York', but the traditional numbers he performed were brilliantly executed, highly original interpretations (with the exception of 'House Of The Rising Sun', which he stole note for note from Dave Van Ronk, thus rupturing their friendship for some months). But even as he was recording them, they were already part of his past.

The same month that the album came out, the first issue of Pete Seeger's *Broadside* magazine was published, dedicated to songs about radical politics, social injustice and racial inequality. While Dylan was scarcely unaware of what was going on about him, two other factors were at work: he had become disillusioned with Woody Guthrie (some have suggested that Guthrie deliberately showed his worst side to Dylan to break his hero-worship); and, through Suze, who was then working as a secretary for the Congress for Racial Equality, he was becoming increasingly aware of the problems faced by black people.

Mixed up confusion

It has been said – not least by Dylan himself – that his espousal of radical causes at this time was purely opportunistic. But it seems more likely that his unstoppable creative energy simply fastened on to what was, in that milieu, unavoidable; and he became politically aware at the very moment that he gained confidence as a writer, knowing at the same time that the idiom of Guthrie could no longer serve him. It is possible, too, that his radicalism was not simply shared with Suze, but became a way to show her that, despite their storms and rages, he was still on her side. But there seems to be no reason to believe that Dylan's public political stance was actually insincere.

In April 1962 he wrote 'Blowin' In The Wind', which became a civil rights anthem and made Dylan impossible to ignore. Over the next year he wrote a mass of topical songs, many of which fell by the wayside, while others were still surfacing on record nearly two years later. His first single was released in December: of all things, it was a rocker, 'Mixed Up Confusion' – a bizarre reversion to his Little Richard persona – and Dylan claims that Columbia disliked it because it clashed with his growing reputation as a 'movement' troubadour; at any rate, it was soon withdrawn.

Meanwhile, Albert Grossman was quietly taking over Dylan's management, and less quietly pushing his songs to other singers under his wing, notably Odetta and Peter, Paul and Mary. By the time *The Freewheelin' Bob Dylan* was released in May 1963, Dylan's name and music were known far beyond Greenwich Village. Though it contained classic period material like 'Masters Of War', 'Talking World War III Blues' and 'Oxford Town', two things stood out from the LP that served as pointers to the future – his persistent use of traditional material even when dealing with the most immediate issues, and the extraordinary quality of his verse.

Two months after the release of *Freewheelin'* Dylan appeared at the Newport Folk Festival and was there pronounced the prophet of the youth revolution, folk division. The 46,000-strong crowd couldn't get enough of him; when he sang 'Blowin' In The Wind', Joan Baez, Pete Seeger, Theo Bikel, Peter, Paul and Mary and sundry others were unable to resist joining him on stage, the impromptu choir moving straight on to 'We Shall Overcome' with everyone joining hands. Dylan came away from Newport a star.

But he was already uncomfortable with the role he had had thrust on him. At the civil rights march on Washington in August, Dylan sang and then nodded toward Capitol Hill and said: 'They ain't listening at all.' His personal life was in confusion: for the second time, Suze had left him, and he was drawing close to Joan Baez. And he was overwhelmed by success and money from record royalties.

By October he had completed another album, *The Times They Are A-Changin'*. It made him ever more the darling of the new Left, but its so-called 'protest' songs were a very far cry from the histrionic generalities of his contemporaries. While they were busy working up a prejudice against Southern whites, Dylan sang 'Only A Pawn In Their Game'; while the Left went liber-

al on criminals, he pointed out their confusion in 'Hattie Carroll'; and in 'North Country Blues' and 'The Ballad Of Hollis Brown' he concentrated on the personal, specific suffering of the protagonists, who thus became universal, mythic victims. And he blamed no one for their plight – it was simply the way of the world. In ending the album with 'Restless Farewell' – 'for myself and my friends my stories are sung . . . I'll bid farewell and not give a damn' – he could hardly have made it plainer that he had to follow his own artistic conscience, not a doctrine, trend or even spokesmen like Guthrie and Pete Seeger.

But by January 1964 Dylan was in a grim state, totally self-centred and isolated from many of his old friends by an entourage of drug fiends dubbed the 'mindguards'. He took off on a six-week odyssey by car to California (ostensibly to play a concert), and when he got back Suze

walked out for the last time. Dylan retreated into himself, and over the next year produced not only the songs on *Another Side Of Bob Dylan* (including the stunning 'To Ramona', 'It Ain't Me, Babe' and his first public hint at mysticism, 'Chimes Of Freedom') but the epics that make up the acoustic half of *Bringing It All Back Home* ('It's Alright, Ma (I'm Only Bleeding)', 'Mr Tambourine Man', 'Gates Of Eden' and 'It's All Over Now, Baby Blue').

Mind-blowing music
Dylan went to England in May for a concert tour, and met the Beatles and Eric Burdon of the Animals. His reaction to the latter's 'House Of The Rising Sun' was enthusiastic, to say the least: 'Totally *wild!* Blew my mind!' Just as Dylan was trying to find a new identity, it became apparent that his first love, rock'n'roll

semble that included Bruce Langhorne on guitar – were the result not only of Dylan's recognition that the rising British bands had put new blood into rock, but also of hearing his own 'Mr Tambourine Man' rendered by the Byrds. Whereas Dylan took up rock because it was appropriate to his art, many of his audience – and all of the purist folk establishment – regarded it as a sell-out to commercialism, a weird leap at becoming a teen idol. And, to their further horror, it was now that Dylan began to assail the US national pop charts.

'Subterranean Homesick Blues', from *Bringing It All Back Home*, reached Number 39 in April while the classic 'Like A Rolling Stone' took him into the Top Ten for the first time three months later, peaking at Number 2. A song of raging hatred, 'Positively 4th Street', gave Dylan his third American hit of the year, reaching Number 7 in October. In Britain, meanwhile, Dylan enjoyed even greater pop success, entering the charts in 1965 on five occasions with 'Times They Are A-

of the old guard's outlook had been unmistakably demonstrated by Pete Seeger as he opened that final evening concert. He played a tape of a newborn baby crying, and suggested that the world in which that child would grow up was an unhappy place, full of poverty, pollution, war and injustice. But tonight's singers, he said, would show that *we shall overcome*.

Electric demons

When the Paul Butterfield Band set up on stage to back Dylan, they had themselves already been cast as electric demons by the folk 'mafia'. The previous day folklorist Alan Lomax had introduced them with the sneer, 'Let's find out if these guys can play at all,' whereupon Albert Grossman entertained the assembled company by busting Lomax in the nose. So it was not surprising, if none the less ludicrous, that as they helped Dylan roar out his great hymn to self-reliance, 'Like A Rolling Stone', Pete Seeger should grab an axe from somewhere and shriek at Grossman: 'I am going

music, could serve his unique vision. His audience seemed quite prepared to let him do whatever he wanted, though his new style dismayed the old guard of folk. They were edgy at Newport in 1964, and reviewers denounced *Another Side* when it came out.

If *Another Side* had displeased these listeners, they were extremely unhappy about *Bringing It All Back Home*. Recorded in early 1965, the rock tracks – on which Dylan was backed by a small en-

Bob Dylan espouses electricity. Right: At the Newport Folk Festival in 1965, Dylan's electric band (with Mike Bloomfield, left, on guitar) incurred the wrath of the purist audience. Above: On stage with the Band at the Woody Guthrie Memorial Concert, Carnegie Hall, 1968. Left and below: Dylan in the studio, 1965.

Changin'', 'Subterranean Homesick Blues', 'Like A Rolling Stone', 'Positively Fourth Street' (all Top Ten entries) and 'Maggie's Farm', which made Number 22.

1965 also saw the release of Dylan's first fully rock-orchestrated album, *Highway 61 Revisited*. Produced in New York by Bob Johnston with backing, again, from Kooper, Bloomfield, Gregg and others, the LP was a quite devastating set – one that many consider to be Dylan's finest moment – which included 'Like A Rolling Stone' along with slabs of R&B ('Tombstone Blues', 'From A Buick 6' and 'Highway 61 Revisited'), the gentle swing of 'It Takes A Lot To Laugh, It Takes A Train To Cry' and the doom-laden sprawl of 'Desolation Row'.

'Desolation Row' vividly revealed that Dylan saw the world not only as horrible but incurably so; and it was this intuition as much as the din he was making with his electric guitar that so upset the complacent liberalism of the folk establishment, and brought about the disaster that was Newport in 1965. The sentimentality

to chop the power cables if you don't take them off the stage right now!' In the event Dylan walked off in tears.

It was not as if Dylan had turned his back on the world, as the folk 'mafia' thought: the stark and unnerving new poetry he wrote, along with his frequently unorthodox harmonic approach, reflected the same insane world that Seeger saw (and often with the same arrogance that Seeger displayed in, say, 'Little Boxes'). But Dylan did not know how to change it. Now that he was famous at last, he couldn't even face the clawing fans: how could he set himself up as their 'leader'? He could only be true to himself. As he stormed at a *Time* reporter in *Don't Look Back* (D. A. Pennebaker's documentary film of Dylan's 1965 British tour): 'I'm saying that you're gonna die, you're gonna go off the Earth, you're gonna be *dead*. . . . And so'm I . . . Alright, now you do your job in the face of that, and however seriously you take yourself, you decide for yourself. Okay, now I'll decide for myself.'

Take three girls: idyllic days with Suze Rotolo (below); joining hands with Joan Baez at the Newport Folk Festival in 1963 (left) and later (far left), and enjoying 'one more cup of coffee' with his wife Sara (above).

Ladies and liars

By the middle of 1965, Dylan was touring with a new band providing the backing. The Hawks (later the Band) – Robbie Robertson, Garth Hudson, Rick Danko and Richard Manuel (augmented by Mickey Jones on drums) – were a remarkably accomplished outfit; they had played together for years, knew each other's musical language inside out and were thus able to provide an ideal backdrop for Dylan's sometimes undisciplined rock numbers. But Dylan's stage performances still managed to arouse the rage of folk purists: when he appeared at London's Albert Hall in 1966, sections of the audience (who, one might assume, should have known from the previous year's succession of rock hits what to expect) were prompted to shriek 'Judas!' Dylan's reply was typically scathing: 'I don't believe you. You're a liar.'

In May 1966, Dylan's seventh album, *Blonde On Blonde* (a double), was released. The LP was produced in Nashville – again by Bob Johnston – and the session musicians included such stalwarts of the country and western scene as Wayne Moss, Charlie McCoy, Kenny Buttrey and Hargus Robbins as well as Kooper and Robbie Robertson. *Blonde On Blonde* was, once more, quite stunning, ranging from the swooping commerciality of 'I Want You' (a Number 20 single hit in the US, Number 16 in Britain), to the beautiful and lengthy 'Sad Eyed Lady Of The Lowlands', generally thought to be a tribute to Sara Lowndes (who Dylan had married on 22 November 1965), from the batty humour of 'Rainy Day Women # 12 & 35' and 'Leopard-Skin Pill-Box Hat' to the despair of 'Visions Of Johanna' on which Dylan stated: 'Name me someone that's not a parasite and I'll go out and say a prayer for him.'

The album had been out for a mere two months when, on 30 July 1966, Bob Dylan fell off his motorcycle near his home in Woodstock and almost died. But the accident proved to be something of a blessing in disguise, for it put an end to the endless touring, the drug abuse and the savagery Dylan inflicted on others. Staring death in the face, he had to make sense of his life or acknowledge that it had been wasted. And this experience was to produce some of his greatest songs.

Dylan spent much of his lengthy convalescence with the Band – now with Levon Helm on drums – in Woodstock. The Band by now were evolving a specific style of their own, an idiosyncratic blend of country music, blues, cajun and folk elements and naturally traded musical – and lyrical – ideas with Dylan. The music he made with them in these months (much of which surfaced in 1975 on the *Basement Tapes* album) was quite unlike the fashionable stuff of the day, although the music revolution of the mid Sixties had his *Highway 61 Revisited* and *Blonde On Blonde* for its mother and midwife. These compositions comprised a mixture of often hilarious, surreal songs such as 'Clothes Line', 'Get Your Rocks Off' and 'Open The Door, Homer' that were musings of one sort or another on absurdity and, in direct contrast, a group of anguished, conscience-stricken meditations on guilt, pain and wrongdoing: 'Tears of Rage', 'Too Much Of Nothing' and the elusive and largely indecipherable 'I'm Not There, I'm Gone'. It is the latter songs that point in the direction of *John Wesley Harding*; in them Dylan began, as he put it in his book *Tarantula*, to 'travel on a slow ship back to your guilt, your pollution, the kingdom of your blues', and recognised his *own* unlovely responsibilities and shortcomings.

New morning dawns

On 20 January 1968, Dylan made his first public appearance since his accident when, backed by the Band, he performed at Carnegie Hall in a memorial concert to Woody Guthrie who had passed away the previous October. And that same month his long-awaited follow-up to *Blonde On Blonde* emerged. *John Wesley Harding* was a startling departure from his previous rock style. Recorded in Nashville with a small core of backing musicians – Charlie McCoy (bass), Kenny Buttrey (drums) and Pete Drake (pedal steel) – the album was remarkably simple and unadorned, completely out of step with the experimental nature of late Sixties rock.

John Wesley Harding was full of biblical references, but despite these Dylan did not look for comfort in religious faith. That is not to say that he was *without* faith; indeed it was after this that he returned to Judaism. In keeping with the recognition of human frailty, not least his own, and of the inevitable recurrence of moral struggle, it was appropriate that he should perceive human, not divine, love as the difficult but fitting expression of life's bounty. And so the album ended with Dylan, for the first time in his life, singing two completely committed and unqualified love songs, 'Down Along The Cove' and 'I'll Be Your Baby Tonight'.

In the autumn of 1968, Dylan flew to Nashville with the expressed intention of recording a country and western album; the resulting *Nashville Skyline*, released in April the following year, was met with much critical apprehension. Although some critics attempted to discern genius in such lines as 'Love to spend the night with Peggy Day', the album was simply light and happy C&W. Despite the exuberance and professionalism of the performances there was little in them to inspire real interest.

Dylan's voice had undergone a dramatic change; it was now softer and had lost much of its harsh nasal quality. Some suggested that the bike accident had affected Dylan's vocal chords, while Dylan himself claimed that the change had been caused by giving up smoking. (Some cynics even propounded the theory that the real Dylan had, in fact, died in the accident and Columbia Records had replaced him with a lookalike.)

Self Portrait, a double album released the following June, was even more of a disappointment than *Nashville Skyline*. It was a hodge-podge of old material, quirky oddities and pop standards, a careless assembly that suggested that Dylan had little more to say. And after the release of *New Morning* in October – an album that was, at least, well-received – the devoted and contented family man was relatively silent for three years.

Shelter from the storm
In 1971 Dylan appeared at George Harrison's Bangladesh benefit concert, where he sang 'Blowin' In The Wind', 'Mr Tambourine Man', 'A Hard Rain's A-Gonna Fall' and other early songs; later in the year he released a single, 'George Jackson', the subject being a black convict who had been killed by prison guards. It reached Number 33 in the US in December and seemed to signal a return to the commitment of earlier years, but throughout 1972 and 1973 he remained somewhat in the shadows. He played the part of Alias in

Sam Peckinpah's *Pat Garrett And Billy The Kid* and also composed the music for the film. The title song was a brilliant portrayal of the outlaw's alienation: the intensity of the poetry and the ingenious use of the blues to carry it showed that Dylan had not lost touch with his creative springs and a powerful single lifted from the soundtrack, 'Knockin' On Heaven's Door', made the Top Twenty on both sides of the Atlantic.

Then on 3 January 1974 Dylan returned to the stage, starting off a major tour in Chicago. Backed by the Band, he played 39 concerts in 25 cities before some three quarters of a million people, mixing songs from all stages of his career into each set. And just as the tour was starting out, his first official album since *New Morning* was released by Asylum Records, Dylan's new label; entitled *Planet Waves*, it featured him backed once more by the Band. The musical performances were stronger and more intense than anything since *Blonde On Blonde* and the LP could be seen as an exploration of his love for Sara in terms of

Dylan's charismatic live performances have been caught on four albums: Before The Flood *(1974),* Hard Rain *(1976),* At The Budokan *(1979) and* Real Live *(1984).*

his past. For the next five years Dylan was to struggle with his attempt to find salvation in love – and specifically in Sara, without whom he could not wholly live but whose love 'cuts like a knife'.

Planet Waves restored Dylan to critical acclaim and also showed that he was still a highly commercial force – the album topped the US charts for three weeks in a row for the first time in Dylan's career. It was followed by a double live album, *Before The Flood*, which marked the end of Dylan's short sojourn on Asylum. At the end of 1974, he returned to Columbia Records in time for *Blood On The Tracks*, a record that truly reasserted the man's genius. His relationship with Sara was deteriorating and the pain and desperation were splattered all over the record. 'Idiot Wind' completely reversed the optimism of 'Blowin' In The Wind': a catalogue of

stupidities and insensitivities, it shifted from a blistering attack on Sara to an admission of mutual lack of imagination. On 'Shelter From The Storm' he says: 'I bargained for salvation/And she gave me a lethal dose', in a bizarre if prophetic identification with the martyred Christ. Nonetheless, though that shelter has a leaky roof, it's all there is and the faith remains that it will endure despite the anguish.

Hard rain and hurricanes

Desire (1975) described the further deterioration of the relationship in a series of mythical tales or (reflecting his then-current project, the movie *Renaldo And Clara*) film scripts: many of the songs were co-written with stage director Jacques Levy. The musical arrangements on the album were excellent, from Scarlet Rivera's eccentric violin playing through Dom Cortese's inventive use of the accordion to the work of backing vocalists Emmylou Harris and Ronee Blakley. From the opening track 'Hurricane' (which protested the innocence of accused murderer

boxer Reuben 'Hurricane' Carter) to the final desolate eulogy of 'Sara', the songs all dealt with treachery and betrayal, subjects which Dylan's imagination simply cannot accommodate, however minutely and incisively he portrays it. 'You must forgive me my unworthiness,' he half begs, half demands. 'Oh, Sara, Don't ever leave me, don't ever go.'

But in spirit if not in body, she had. Within a year of the album's release, in February 1977, they formally separated. In June, Bob and Sara Dylan were divorced. Dylan's answer to his pain during this period lay in work; in 1975 and 1976 he had toured the States once more with his Rolling Thunder Revue which included, at various times, Joan Baez, Ronee Blakley, Mick Ronson, Roger McGuinn, Joni Mitchell and Scarlet Rivera. The tour was an immense success, though the live album it yielded, *Hard Rain*, was somewhat patchy. In January 1978 the four-hour *Renaldo And Clara* was released. Shot during the Rolling Thunder Revue, it intercut concert footage with semi-auto-

biographical scenes acted out between Dylan, Sara and Joan Baez and both bored and baffled the critics (it was subsequently cut to a more palatable length). 1978 also saw the release of a new album, *Street-Legal*, on which Dylan can be seen clearly moving towards the religious conversion that was soon to claim him, both in its imagery and in the gospel-like responses of the backing vocalists.

Born again

Dylan's last few albums had been redolent with Christian imagery, so it was no surprise – if still something of a shock – that Dylan should find peace in evangelical Christianity. The albums following his conversion – *Slow Train Coming* (1979), *Saved* (1980) and *Shot Of Love* (1981) – were still musically creative, if over-dependent on sometimes unimaginative session musicians.

Infidels (1983), *Real Live* (1984) and *Empire Burlesque* (1985) met a lukewarm reception, but *Biograph,* a retrospective set, garnered plaudits in early 1986.

Knocked Out Loaded (1986) followed *Infidels* in using an outside producer, Dave Stewart of Eurythmics following Dire Straits' Mark Knopfler. But this failed to stimulate his creativity—a charge equally true of the 1987 film *Hearts of Fire* and the album of mainly cover versions, *Down In The Groove,* that followed it in 1988. But that same year brought reflected glory writing with U2 on their best-selling *Rattle And Hum* LP.

Bob Dylan's achievements remain remarkable: in the Sixties he changed the face, the sound and the meaning of rock music by freeing its potential as an art form. Musicians from the Beatles to the new wave owe him an enormous debt.

P. L. FRANKSON

Above: The Rolling Thunder Revue; from left Roger McGuinn, Arlo Guthrie, Ramblin' Jack Elliott, Joan Baez, Dylan, Mick Ronson, Rob Stoner, Ronee Blakley and Bobby Neuwirth kick out the jams. Right: August 1969, Isle of Wight – Bob tops the bill.

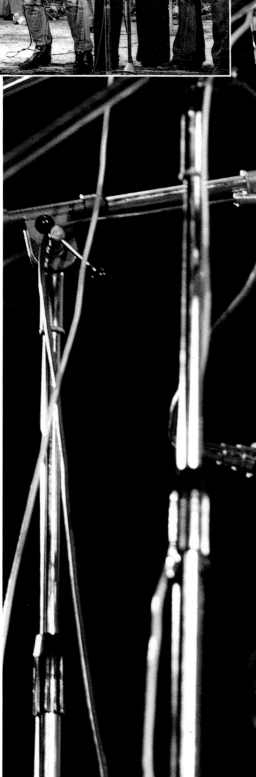

BOB DYLAN
Discography to 1984

Singles
Mixed Up Confusion/Corrina, Corrina (Columbia 42656, 1962); Blowin' In The Wind/Don't Think Twice, It's All Right (Columbia 42856, 1963); Subterranean Homesick Blues/She Belongs To Me (Columbia 43242, 1965); Like A Rolling Stone/Gates Of Eden (Columbia 43346, 1965); Positively 4th Street/From A Buick 6 (Columbia 43389, 1965); Can You Please Crawl Out Your Window/Highway 61 Revisited (Columbia 43477, 1965); One Of Us Must Know (Sooner Or Later)/Queen Jane Approximately (Columbia 43541, 1966); Rainy Day Women # 12 And 35/Pledging My Time (Columbia 43592, 1966); I Want You/Just Like Tom Thumb's Blues (Columbia 43683, 1966); Just Like A Woman/Obviously 5 Believers (Columbia 43792, 1966); Leopard-Skin Pill-Box Hat/Most Likely You Go Your Way And I'll Go Mine (Columbia 44069, 1967); I Threw It All Away/Drifter's Escape (Columbia 44826, 1969); Lay Lady Lay/Peggy Day (Columbia 44926, 1969); Tonight I'll Be Staying Here With You/Country Pie (Columbia 45004, 1969); Wigwam/Copper Kettle (The Pale Moonlight) (Columbia 45199, 1970); Watching The River Flow/Spanish Is The Loving Tongue (Columbia 45409, 1971); George Jackson (acoustic version)/George Jackson (big band version) (Columbia 45516, 1971); Knockin' On Heaven's Door/Turkey Chase (Columbia 45913, 1973); A Fool Such As I/Lily Of The West (Columbia 45982, 1973); On A Night Like This/You Angel You (Asylum 11033, 1974); Something There Is About You/Tough Mama (Asylum 11035, 1974); It Ain't Me Babe/All Along The Watchtower (Asylum 45212, 1974); Tangled Up In Blue/If You See Her, Say Hello (Columbia 10106, 1975); Million Dollar Bash/Tears Of Rage (Columbia 10217, 1976); Hurricane/Hurricane (Part One) (Columbia 10245, 1976); Mozambique/Oh Sister (Columbia 10298, 1976); Rita May/Stuck Inside Of Mobile With The Memphis Blues Again (Columbia 10454, 1977); Baby Stop Crying/New Pony (Columbia 10805, 1978); Changing Of The Guards/Señor (Tales Of Yankee Power) (Columbia 10851, 1978); Gotta Serve Somebody/Trouble In Mind (Columbia 11072, 1979); Man Gave Names To All The Animals/When You Gonna Wake Up (Columbia 11168, 1979); Slow Train/Do Right To Me Baby (Do Unto Others) (Columbia 11235, 1980); Solid Rock/Covenant Woman (Columbia 11318, 1980); Saved/Are You Ready (Columbia 11370, 1980); Groom's Still Waiting At The Altar/Heart Of Mine (Columbia 18-02510, 1980).

Albums
Bob Dylan (Columbia CS8579, 1962); *The Freewheelin' Bob Dylan* (Columbia CS8786, 1963); *The Times They Are A-Changin'* (Columbia CS8905, 1964); *Another Side Of Bob Dylan* (Columbia CS8993, 1964); *Bringing It All Back Home* (Columbia CS9128, 1965); *Highway 61 Revisited* (Columbia CS9189, 1965); *Blonde On Blonde* (Columbia C2L-41, 1966); *Bob Dylan's Greatest Hits* (Columbia KCS9463, 1967); *John Wesley Harding* (Columbia CS9604, 1968); *Nashville Skyline* (Columbia KCS9825, 1969); *Self Portrait* (Columbia C2X30050, 1970); *New Morning* (Columbia KC30290, 1970); *Bob Dylan's Greatest Hits Volume II* (Columbia KC31120, 1971); *Dylan* (Columbia PC32747, 1973); *Planet Waves* (Asylum 7E-1003, 1974); *Before The Flood* (Asylum AB-201, 1974); *Blood On The Tracks* (Columbia PC33235, 1975); *The Basement Tapes* (Columbia CS33682, 1975); *Desire* (Columbia PC33893, 1975); *Hard Rain* (Columbia PC34349, 1976); *Street-Legal* (Columbia JC35453, 1978); *Slow Train Coming* (Columbia FC36120-6, 1979); *At Budokan* (Columbia PC2-36067, 1979); *Saved* (Columbia FC36553, 1980); *Shot Of Love* (Columbia TC37496, 1981); *Infidels* (CBS 25539, 1984); *Real Live* (CBS 26334, 1984).

Conclusions on the Wall

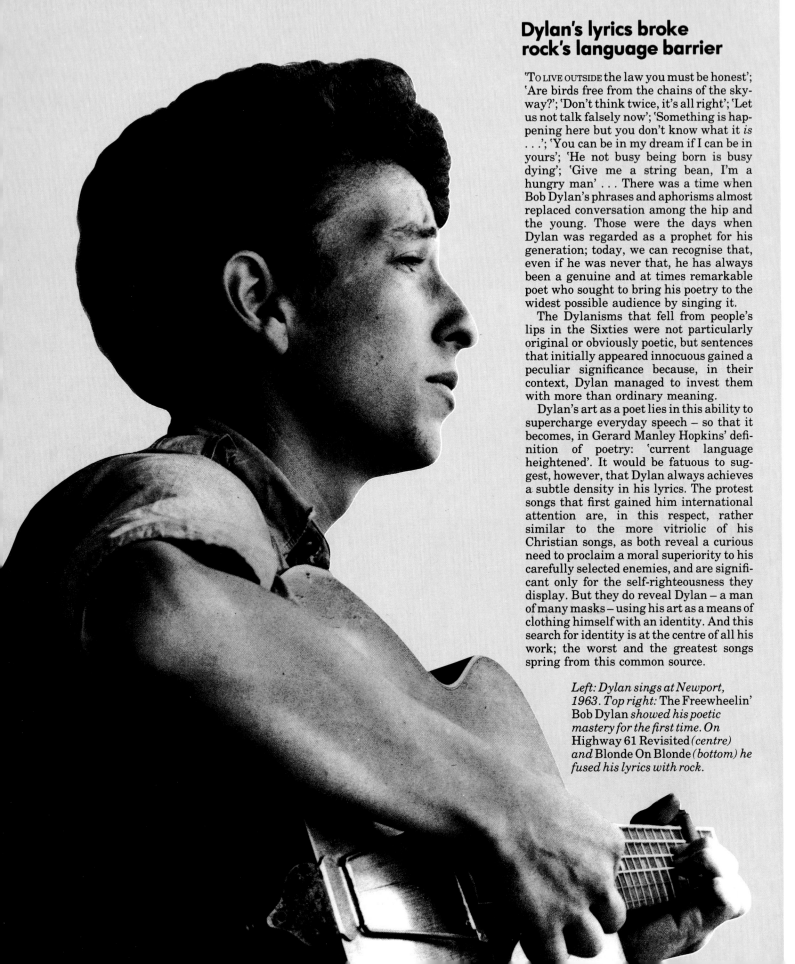

Dylan's lyrics broke rock's language barrier

'To LIVE OUTSIDE the law you must be honest'; 'Are birds free from the chains of the sky-way?'; 'Don't think twice, it's all right'; 'Let us not talk falsely now'; 'Something is happening here but you don't know what it *is* . . .'; 'You can be in my dream if I can be in yours'; 'He not busy being born is busy dying'; 'Give me a string bean, I'm a hungry man' . . . There was a time when Bob Dylan's phrases and aphorisms almost replaced conversation among the hip and the young. Those were the days when Dylan was regarded as a prophet for his generation; today, we can recognise that, even if he was never that, he has always been a genuine and at times remarkable poet who sought to bring his poetry to the widest possible audience by singing it.

The Dylanisms that fell from people's lips in the Sixties were not particularly original or obviously poetic, but sentences that initially appeared innocuous gained a peculiar significance because, in their context, Dylan managed to invest them with more than ordinary meaning.

Dylan's art as a poet lies in this ability to supercharge everyday speech – so that it becomes, in Gerard Manley Hopkins' definition of poetry: 'current language heightened'. It would be fatuous to suggest, however, that Dylan always achieves a subtle density in his lyrics. The protest songs that first gained him international attention are, in this respect, rather similar to the more vitriolic of his Christian songs, as both reveal a curious need to proclaim a moral superiority to his carefully selected enemies, and are significant only for the self-righteousness they display. But they do reveal Dylan – a man of many masks – using his art as a means of clothing himself with an identity. And this search for identity is at the centre of all his work; the worst and the greatest songs spring from this common source.

Left: Dylan sings at Newport, 1963. Top right: The Freewheelin' Bob Dylan *showed his poetic mastery for the first time. On* Highway 61 Revisited *(centre) and* Blonde On Blonde *(bottom) he fused his lyrics with rock.*

This may help explain why Dylan so delights in curious games with words, reversals of the obvious, and rather cryptic 'proverbs'. 'I never asked for your crutch/ Now don't ask for mine' is more than just an easy pun in the context of 'Fourth Time Around', which is largely about the dependence, jealousy and lust that the narrator is all too glad to escape. And while Dylan has often employed clichés ironically ('Love is so simple – to coin a phrase!') or simply because on occasion banality can achieve a kind of mystical simplicity, he can also remake a cliché from scratch. So, instead of saying 'I fell about with mirth' in 'Spanish Harlem Incident', he says 'I got to

laugh halfways off my heels'. But these are relatively superficial tricks of language: the best of Dylan's songs count as poetry because they are greater than the sum of their parts.

Death's pale horse
It took some time for Dylan's art to reach this level of achievement, however. But even if the early protest songs are a lesser part of his achievement, they can still exhibit momentary flashes of extraordinary poetic insight, purely through Dylan's sensitivity to language. Take, for example, 'Masters Of War'; having droned on about the 'masters of war' who 'hide

Above: Blood on the tracks? Twelve years after the release of his first album, Dylan's gift for language continued to amaze.

behind desks' while sending young people off to die, Dylan says 'even Jesus would never forgive what you do': which presumption gives him the licence to hope that their 'death will come soon'. But the stale polemic of the song is transformed by the line 'I'll follow your casket/In the pale afternoon'. The single word 'pale' conjures up the powerful traditional image of Death's pale horse; it is a grim image that suggests something fundamental will have died and thus broadens the line into

one of more universal significance.

Many of Dylan's most successful songs in this period were based on traditional material. 'Bob Dylan's Dream', a requiem for lost friendships, derives from 'Lord Franklin', the lament of a sailor for the explorer Sir John Franklin who died searching for the North-West Passage in 1845. Both songs are concerned with loyalty and loss, and the poignancy of Dylan's lyrics depends to some extent on an awareness of the older ballad. Similarly, 'A Hard Rain's A-Gonna Fall' clearly demonstrates how Dylan's meaning could be intensified in the light of the original material from which it had been adapted. The structure of 'Hard Rain' is based closely on the ballad 'Lord Randal', which employs the technique of question-and-answer in a dialogue between a mother and her son:

Oh where have you been, Lord Randal, my son?
And where have you been, my handsome young son?
I ha' been at the greenwood, now make my bed soon
I'm weary with huntin' and fain would lie doon.

But it also echoes the content of the original: Lord Randal is weary because he has been poisoned by his true love; in 'Hard Rain', it is the whole world that has been poisoned and that is 'sick at the heart' (as the older song puts it). The two-line reply of the original becomes an endless flood of

disconnected images of pain and horror, yoking together opposites and oddities, building up a collage of a world that has gone out of control. There are other influences at work here besides British folk song, most notably the French Symbolist poets whose works Dylan had been introduced to by Suze Rotolo. This debt is most apparent in the songs he wrote between 1964 and 1967, which Dylan said were 'pictures'. This is a characteristic passage from Rimbaud:

As soon as the idea of the Deluge had abated a rabbit stopped in the clover and the swinging bell-flowers and said his prayers through the spider's web to the rainbow, and the flowers were already looking around – but, Oh, the precious stones were hiding themselves ... And the Queen, the Witch, who fires her embers in the broken pot, never wants to tell us what she knows ...

That is mildly reminiscent of parts of Dylan's 'Desolation Row', and Dylan undoubtedly learned much from Rimbaud, Gautier and Mallarmé. But although he used their methods, it was his instinctive feel for the English language that produced lines that had a real resonance, lines like: 'From the crossroads of my doorstep/ My eyes start to fade.' Dylan is also part of the strand of Surrealism native to American culture. Walt Whitman and William Carlos Williams are the respectable end of a line that ends in Lawrence Ferlinghetti and Allen Ginsberg. The latter's *Howl*, as much as anything in French, lies behind much of Dylan's verse at this time. The difference is that Dylan is a better poet than any of the Beats, if only because his precise and specific language is crafted to mean something:

He looks so truthful, is this how he feels
Trying to peel the moon and expose it
With his businesslike anger and his bloodhounds that kneel
If he needs a third eye he just grows it
He just needs you to talk or to hand him his chalk
Or pick it up after he throws it

These lines from 'Can You Please Crawl Out Your Window' are littered with quirky images and incongruous notions for a purpose: they add up to a portrait that potently describes the evil obverse of the self-reliance praised in 'Like A Rolling Stone' in equally exacting language.

Freedom, responsibility, power, and what they mean in a chaotic, murderously threatening world: these are the matters that concerned Dylan at this time – just as, it might be said, they always have; but

Top left: Nashville Skyline, *released in 1970, signalled Dylan's interest in country music, while* Self Portrait *(top right), issued later the same year, seemed to suggest an acute loss of direction. However, 1975's* Desire *(left) and* Street-Legal *(right) in 1978 showed that Dylan's muse had not deserted him.*

because all the answers could so easily be made to seem meaningless, Dylan's songs show disorder and paranoia ruling a shattered landscape of despair and cruelty. All that holds Dylan's vision together is its honesty and integrity in confronting the nightmare, and, even though (in his hate songs – 'Positively Fourth Street', for example) that sometimes means being cruel and nightmarish himself, that is surely an heroic enough achievement.

Echoes of Eliot

In the late Sixties, after Dylan himself had come near to death, he turned to a more sparse, traditional language that owes much to the King James Bible and John Bunyan in describing the profound changes he had experienced. But the songs of *John Wesley Harding* are only superficially simpler than the earlier, metaphor-laden verses. The album recounts a process from overwhelming arrogance, through the dark night of the soul, to renewed purpose and a new wonder in the world. One of the most remarkable songs is 'All Along The Watchtower', which is sung in a curious gapped scale of only four notes and has direct literary echoes of passages from the book of Isaiah, from William Blake's *Jerusalem* and T. S. Eliot.

The song starts with a typically oblique Dylanesque conversation between two mythical characters, the joker and the thief. The joker is confused, abused and

misunderstood, but the thief calms him, saying that many people realise that 'life is but a joke' (which suggests that the joker has some responsibility for the state of affairs he mourns). This is no time for falsehood; 'the hour is getting late.' Next we are shown princes, their women, 'barefoot servants too' while outside the wind begins to howl and nameless riders approach through the gathering storm.

The truths of both the joker and the thief have been disregarded and exploited; how far the exploiters have got from reality is signalled by the abrupt shift of scene in the song to the princes 'all along the watchtower' and something like the Apocalypse, a revolt of nature, seems to be the consequence. Merely protesting at this is not the solution ('Let us not talk falsely now'); salvation, for Dylan, lies in human love, as the album goes on to show. The point to be made about this particular song, however, is that its language contains the maximum of connotative meaning within an extremely terse economy of statement, and for all the literary references, it is entirely original to Dylan. This was Dylan's staple technique during the early Seventies and provided the basis for the few visionary songs he wrote at this time, the movement from loneliness to an ideal of marriage in 'Sign On The Window', for instance, or the

cinematic technique of 'Three Angels' and 'When I Paint My Masterpiece'.

Dylan also uses the technique of juxtaposition to extraordinary effect in 'No Time To Think' (on *Street Legal*), a song marked by a deliberately inane waltz-time and some stunning rhymes. The song presents the chaotic flux of experience, then precisely matches these concrete particulars with a descriptive abstraction, often ironic:

In the Federal City you've been
    blown and shown pity in secret
For pieces of change.
The Empress attracts you but
    oppression distracts you
And it makes you feel violent and
    strange,
Memory, ecstasy,
Tyranny, hypocrisy.

Thought, put like that, is meaningless – 'useless and pointless knowledge'. But it can break through to a new awareness of reality, for the whole verse is summed up in a fresh poetic image:

Betrayed by a kiss on a cool night of
    bliss
In the valley of the missing link
And there's no time to think.

Bob Dylan finds time to think – and write a song (below).

The last line can thus be taken two ways: either that in such a busy world, there *is* no time to think or judge one's actions; or on the other hand the line can be seen as ironic – thought is creative only when tied to the minute particulars of experience, but not to think (to pretend to be unable to think) is cowardice, a deadly abstraction.

From this point in the late Seventies, Dylan spent most of his creative energy expressing his joy in Christ, and it has become a pastime of critics to hold up to the light every reference to Jesus they can find in his earlier work. But all of Dylan's output has been informed by an essentially religious belief that *somewhere* there is meaning and purpose to life in the face of a fallen world and inevitable personal death. It is surprising – indeed unacceptable – to many people that this should preoccupy a singer of rock'n'roll music, but it has been the traditional function of the artist. In Dylan's case it has taken many forms, from bald social comment to varieties of tenderness and savagery in his dealings with women, while his techniques are as varied as the subjects to which he has addressed himself. Dylan has shown that it is still possible to write poetry in modern English. That is no mean achievement for a man whose ambition was once no more than 'to join Little Richard'.   PETER BROOKESMITH

Bringing It All Back Home

The influences on Dylan and those he inspired

ANY CONSIDERATION of the influence of Bob Dylan on the history of rock music has to take into account the formative influences on Dylan himself. Throughout his career, there has been a two-way traffic of ideas between Dylan and other individual performers and areas of popular music. Running parallel to Dylan's love of the folk tradition of Woody Guthrie was his devotion to early rock'n'roll; his formative years were a rich mix of Hank Williams, the Everly Brothers, Leadbelly, James Dean, Johnny Ace, Jack Kerouac and Lord Buckley. A heady combination of comics, rock'n'rollers, country stars and R&B singers.

Indeed, Dylan's first projected single, recorded in 1962, was a healthy slab of rockabilly called 'Mixed Up Confusion', which was withdrawn shortly after its release as CBS felt it didn't fit their image of Dylan as a troubled troubadour. His first LP, entitled simply *Bob Dylan*, drew heavily on the folk and country blues traditions; while 'Highway 51' came from the blues tradition, 'Gospel Plow' was an old spiritual and 'House Of The Rising Sun' a traditional number learned from fellow folk singer Dave Van Ronk. 'Song To Woody' was, of course, dedicated to Dylan's idol Woody Guthrie, while the album's closing number, 'See That My Grave Is Kept Clean' was a powerful blues by Blind Lemon Jefferson.

From blues to the Beatles
It is a measure of Dylan's innovative talent that the successive fields of music, such as folk, electric rock and country and western, which he entered at each stage of his career, were transformed by his contribution to them. In his early songs, he relied on simple acoustic guitar accompaniment and focused on specific incidents, as in 'The Ballad Of Donald White' and 'The Death Of Emmett Till'. It was his later, more abstract protest songs like 'Blowin' In The Wind', 'When The Ship Comes In' and 'Only A Pawn In Their Game' that exerted such a strong influence on his Greenwich Village contemporaries.

Although Dylan himself didn't hit the charts until 1965, his influence was apparent long before. Peter, Paul and Mary's version of 'Blowin' In The Wind' reached Number 2 in America in 1963, and Joan Baez made a point of including many Dylan songs in her repertoire. Dylan's influence on the Beatles was apparent early in their career. John Lennon particularly was impressed with the honesty Dylan incorporated in his lyrics, and began to include 'Dylanesque' sentiments in songs like 'I'm A Loser' and 'Baby's In Black' on the 1964 *Beatles For Sale* album. Lennon's interest continued on the *Help!* and *Rubber Soul* albums with songs like 'You've Got To Hide Your Love Away' and 'Norwegian Wood'.

Talented writers like Phil Ochs, Tom Paxton, Richard Farina, Paul Clayton and David Blue were amazed at Dylan's precocious ability to translate topical incidents into songs of lyrical beauty. The prolificity of that material was only matched by its high quality. But Dylan was always too much of a chameleon to stay in any one place for too long. While others – such as Barry McGuire, Donovan and Sonny Bono – edged their way onto the 'protest' bandwagon, Dylan had moved on. A willingness to experiment and a refusal to be pigeonholed have remained constant in an otherwise mercurial career.

Dylan plugs in
Dylan realised the possibilities of 'folk-rock' as early as 1964 when he heard how the Animals had treated the traditional 'House Of The Rising Sun'. The Byrds weren't slow off the mark to realise the commercial potential of Dylan's material. Their truncated version of 'Mr Tambourine Man' was a global hit, a timeless summer anthem that ensured the composer's name was on every hip lip.

With his classic *Bringing It All Back Home* album in 1965, Dylan took one giant leap for rock'n'roll, fusing vivid, surreal lyrics with the raw power of rock rhythms. During that incredibly fertile period, bordered by *Bringing It All Back Home* and *Blonde On Blonde*, Dylan's influence was

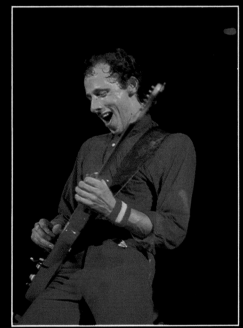

Insets, clockwise from bottom: Eric Burdon of the Animals, whose 'House Of The Rising Sun' made Dylan realise folk-rock's potential; Dire Straits' Mark Knopfler, who borrowed his vocal style from Dylan; James Dean, a prime influence on Dylan's image; and Willie Nelson, whose 'Outlaw' country was inspired greatly by Nashville Skyline.

universal. His young disciples gazed awe-struck at his progress – Paul Simon, Neil Young, Van Morrison, Jackson Browne, James Taylor and Joni Mitchell were only some who were overwhelmed by Dylan's style, and began their imitative efforts.

In electrifying his music, Dylan did more than just set a fashion for other musicians; he conferred a legitimacy on a form of music still regarded with profound suspicion by the aficionados of 'serious' music such as folk. Into a dream world of beach parties and surfing safaris, Dylan proffered the reality of genuine emotion, persecution and segregation. His example was to be crucial for the musical upheavals of the late Sixties and for the new generation of rock fans who saw their music as sharply distinct from 'pop', and demanded intelligent music and literate lyrics rather than chirpy celebrations of teenage love.

Travellin' on ...
But Dylan, as usual, was one step ahead of his fans. While they were assimilating his new 'rock' phase, and while rock itself was going psychedelic, Dylan was spending his convalescence from a motorcycle accident recording a large body of country music with the Band at their house in upstate New York. Bootlegs aside, this material didn't surface until *The Basement Tapes* was released in 1975, but the fruits of this musical exploration were apparent on the 1968 LP *John Wesley Harding*. Tracks like 'I'll Be Your Baby Tonight' helped pave the way for the remarkable Gram Parsons/Byrds *Sweetheart Of The Rodeo* country-rock album. The following year, Dylan plunged deeper into C&W with his own *Nashville Skyline*, an album that was an unashamed celebration of the then un-fashionable country music. It set the seal of approval on C&W for a whole new, young generation, laying a foundation for the country-rock of the Eagles, Linda Ronstadt, Commander Cody, Joe Ely and the 'Outlaw' country of Waylon Jennings and Willie Nelson.

A three-year period of near-silence followed *New Morning* in 1970. With the advent of the singer/songwriter vogue of the early Seventies, personified by the success of James Taylor and Carole King, Dylan was regarded as one of rock's elder statesmen. His name was never far from the headlines, particularly during the music press's quest for 'the new Dylan'.

Such performers as Bruce Springsteen, John Prine, Steve Goodman, Steve Forbert and Loudon Wainwright III were lumbered with this unpromising epithet. For nearly all, it did more harm than good, and few sustained their early promise. Even Springsteen's 1973 debut album, *Greetings From Asbury Park NJ*, had Dylan stamped all over it – particularly 'Blinded By The Light', which bore an uncanny resemblance to Dylan's 'Subterranean Homesick Blues' of eight years before.

By the mid-Seventies, it was arguable that Dylan's influence was negligible. But, true to form, he was continuing to look

The Band's last concert in 1976 united Dylan with several disciples. Joni Mitchell, Neil Young and Van Morrison joined Dylan, Dr John (left) and Band bassist Rick Danko (third from right) on stage.

around him, absorbing new influences and synthesising older ones. *Blood On The Tracks* (1974) and *Desire* (1975) saw him fusing folk, country, Tex-Mex and even traditional Jewish religious music into a subtle and mature vehicle for personal expression. Although the introspective cast of these albums seems to reflect the singer-songwriter boom that Dylan himself did so much to spark off, they stood aside from the work of many of his contemporaries in their harrowing honesty and avoidance of self-pity.

The next generation
As part of the rock establishment, Dylan could not remain immune from the punk backlash of the mid to late Seventies. Nevertheless, his influence on a younger generation of musicians was still noticeable. A young Elvis Costello could be heard crooning 'Knocking On Heaven's Door', a song also included in the live set of New York new wave band Television; Dire Straits' Mark Knopfler borrowed much of his vocal phrasing from Dylan – and later played guitar on *Slow Train Coming* – and the militant Tom Robinson Band included 'I Shall Be Released' at virtually every gig. (The song was later adapted as the official anthem of Amnesty International.)

Dylan then turned his attention to gospel music on his 1978 LP *Street-Legal*. With a big backing band and a trio of female vocalists echoing his lyrics, call-and-response style, this testifying album prefigured Dylan's conversion to Christianity the following year. A series of desul-

tory evangelistic albums which followed displayed Dylan's continuing preoccupation with soul music: for *Slow Train Coming*, he called in the services of Jerry Wexler, who had produced many of Atlantic's great soul artists of the Sixties, while Donald 'Duck' Dunn, the famous Stax bassist, contributed to *Shot Of Love*.

Although it is his earlier work which has had the most impact on the course of rock music, that impact has been incalculable. Indeed, a survey of the artists who have recorded Dylan songs provides an indication of his standing. A random selection reveals Elvis Presley, Rod Stewart, Eric Clapton, Bryan Ferry, Johnny Cash and Manfred Mann. The Hollies, Joan Baez and Coulson, Dean, McGuinness, Flint have recorded entire albums of Dylan songs. David Bowie put his own tribute, 'Song For Bob Dylan', on 1971's *Hunky Dory*, and Jimi Hendrix proved how far a Dylan song could be stretched when he transformed 'All Along The Watchtower' into a seething electric vision of the Apocalypse.

Dylan's durability is evident in the scope of his influence and the breadth of his musical vision; the scope of his song styles has been an inspiration to countless musicians, and rock music has been irrevocably changed by his input. PATRICK HUMPHRIES

Blues and More...

How differing talents flowered from a common blues root

THE TERM 'progressive blues' has always been something of a misnomer when applied to R&B-influenced rock music of the late Sixties and early Seventies. A true definition is virtually impossible, as the tag covers such a hybrid mix of individuals, ranging from Steve Miller on the West Coast to Johnny Winter in Texas to Jeff Beck in London. They meet on one piece of common ground: a love for the blues as defined by the black community of Chicago in the late Fifties and early Sixties. Bluesmen like Muddy Waters, B. B. King, Buddy Guy, Little Walter, Otis Rush and Freddie King, all played regularly at clubs and theatres in Chicago throughout that period. The postwar years saw a massive influx of blacks into the city, seeking work in car factories and steel mills. Bars and night-clubs mushroomed, all featuring this new, embryonic music. By 1955, the acoustic, lyrical blues of Mississippi and surrounding Southern states had gone for good, replaced by amplified rhythm and blues music. A string of small record companies had sprung up, spearheaded by Chess on South Michigan Avenue. Its roster included Chuck Berry, Bo Diddley, Muddy Waters, Little Walter, Otis Rush, Buddy Guy, Howlin' Wolf, Sonny Boy Williamson and Elmore James.

By the early Sixties a musical and sociological pattern had emerged; it was this street-level appeal that attracted many young white rock musicians to the blues in both the States and Britain – many moved to Chicago to discover more about the lifestyle that spawned the music and a flourishing scene soon evolved. Paul Butterfield, Steve Miller, Johnny Winter, Mike Bloomfield, Charlie Musselwhite, Barry Goldberg, Harvey Mandel, Elvin Bishop and John Hammond Jr were all in at the beginning. Butterfield grew up in Chicago and studied classical flute in his youth. By the time he reached his teens, he had settled for harmonica, sitting in with blues artists on the South Side. He formed his first group in 1958 at the age of 16, recruiting Elvin Bishop into his band in 1962 and Mike Bloomfield two years later.

Steve Miller, born in Wisconsin but raised in Texas, claims he learnt guitar by repeatedly playing one favourite single: Bill Doggett's 'Honky Tonk', a Number 1 R&B instrumental in 1956. 'I was entranced by his guitar player . . . I don't even know the guy's name,' he later admitted. (Doggett was a jazz organist from Philadelphia, and his guitarist was Billy Butler.) Before hitting Chicago, Miller led a Top Forty band called the Ardells, which included guitarist Boz Scaggs. Miller started jamming with the big names before joining the Charlie Musselwhite Band. Musselwhite was a 20-year-old white harmonica-player, born in Mississippi, later moving to Memphis where he grew up listening to local blues veterans like Furry Lewis and the Memphis Jug Band. Other

members of his Chicago group included Barry Goldberg, (keyboards) who later joined the Electric Flag, and drummer Eddie Hoh (featured on the Al Kooper/Mike Bloomfield *Super Session* album). The music was straight R&B with no frills; plenty of Elmore James, Albert Kink, Magic Sam and, of course, Little Walter. Musselwhite, like Butterfield, was heavily influenced by the deep, resonant sound of Walter's amplified harmonica and his contribution to the success of Muddy Waters' early records cannot be overstated. (Walter led a violent life, his death in 1968 resulting from injuries received in a fight.)

Miller and Goldberg quit Musselwhite in the summer of 1965 to form their own band, working regularly in such clubs as the Hideaway, Pepper's and the C&J Lounge. Over on the West Coast, the psychedelic movement was underway. Boz Scaggs had moved to San Fran-

Otis Rush was just one of many bluesmen to record for Chicago's Chess label, a company instrumental in introducing the sound of black electric blues to white ears.

In the Sixties the black sound of Chicago was adopted by many white Americans. Among these were guitarists Johnny Winter (left) and Harvey Mandel (top left) and groups like the Goldberg-Miller Blues Band (top right) and the Blues Project (above). Meanwhile, black singer Taj Mahal (right) progressed from blues to Third World flirtations.

cisco, encouraging Miller to do the same. He eventually arrived in late 1966, forming the Steve Miller Band with Scaggs on dual lead guitar. Success was soon to follow.

Fickle Pickle

This was the era of Ken Kesey's Merry Pranksters, the San Francisco Mime Troupe and Bill Graham's Fillmore West. Things had started to happen in 1965 when the Byrds took up a residency at a North Beach night club, the Peppermint Tree. Suddenly there was a proliferation of new bands: the Grateful Dead, Jefferson Airplane, Big Brother and the Holding Company, Country Joe and the Fish and the Quicksilver Messenger Service. While Steve Miller was working the Chicago South Side circuit, Johnny Winter was over on the West Side with a residency at the Fickle Pickle, a blues/folk lounge then run by Mike Bloomfield. Several other white blues performers emerged from that extraordinarily productive Chicago scene of the early Sixties. John Hammond Jr was a prominent figure; a singer/guitarist of some intensity, he recorded a spate of albums for Vanguard Records – perhaps wisely, as his father was a key executive at Columbia, signing both Bob Dylan and Janis Joplin.

Harvey Mandel was another early resident in Chicago. Born in Detroit, he joined one of Charlie Musselwhite's many musical aggregations. Perhaps surprisingly, Mandel's first major solo album, the futuristic 1968 release, *Cristo Redentor*, owed nothing to the traditional blues form. In 1970 he joined Canned Heat for a short period, before embarking on a progressive jazz career. One final outfit deserves mention in this brief look at white Chicago R&B – the Siegel/Schwall Band. Although they recorded half-a-dozen albums of raw R&B – mostly for Vanguard – the band remained unknown outside the States. Back in the mid Sixties, Corky Siegel's harmonica and Jim Schwall's lead guitar held all the promise of greater things. By 1970, however, they had moved to San Francisco, where they fell into a rapid, yet bizarre decline that climaxed with an appearance at the local opera house as 'guest artists' with the San Francisco Symphony Orchestra.

While the Chicago blues scene blossomed, its New York equivalent remained fairly lacklustre. Most of the musicians emerged from the Greenwich Village folk revival of the early Sixties, and their attempts at performing solid R&B were generally uninspired. The Blues Project, formed and originally fronted by Al Kooper, turned out to be a huge disappointment outside its hometown following. Their debut Verve album, *Live At The Cafe Au Go Go*, was acclaimed by local critics – even though it contained thin versions of Chicago R&B standards like 'Spoonful' and 'Back Door Man'. Another New York singer/guitarist, Taj Mahal, gained something of a cult following when he moved to California in the mid Sixties. Only Robert Cray, a Georgia-born black singer/guitarist in his thirties whose albums dented the US and UK charts in 1987 and 1988, waved the flag for electric blues in the Eighties.

DAVE WALTERS

SPACE

COWBOY

The many faces of the irrepressible Steve Miller

IF ROCK AND THEATRE have their parallels, then Steve Miller must be classed as one of music's character actors. A self-styled space cowboy, country picker and midnight toker, he is one of the few artists of the West Coast acid rock period to remain relevant in the Eighties. The key to his longevity has been his songs, which have combined a confidential intimacy with a rare humour, their seeming simplicity belied by the chuckle in the delivery: is he laughing *with* the listener or *at* him? After a fifteen-year recording career and a performing history of nearly twice that, Steve Miller remained an infuriating – yet likeable – enigma in the Eighties.

Aboard the Night Train

Born in Milwaukee, Wisconsin, on 5 November 1943, Steve Miller spent his early life in Texas. Although his father was a doctor, he grew up in a musical environment; his mother had been a singer, and legendary guitar pioneer Les Paul was a family friend. Little wonder, then, that both Steve and younger brother Jim took up the guitar, and by the time Steve had reached his teens, the two were playing together in the six-piece Marksman Combo with another youngster, William 'Boz' Scaggs.

The elder Miller and Scaggs enrolled at the University of Madison, Wisconsin, in 1961, continuing their after-hours partnership in a white-soul band called the Ardells – the personnel of which formed the basis of the Night Train, a cabaret band, in the summer vacation. Miller's prowess on guitar and harmonica made music a possible career and, after a further year's study in Copenhagen, he moved to Chicago. The next step was a period of 'paying dues' in the backing bands of sundry blues legends then on the city's club circuit, Buddy Guy and Muddy Waters among them.

A musical direction now established, Steve teamed with Barry Goldberg to form a blues band that gigged for some months under their joint names. According to Miller, the band 'was offered 11 recording contracts the first set it ever played', and the one they accepted was with Epic Records. But management problems and the unsympathetic attitude of Epic caused Steve to quit the band after the release of one single 'Mother Song' (though a second single, 'Ginger Man', appeared much later).

Disillusioned, Steve Miller returned to Texas, taking a job as caretaker at a Fort Worth recording studio where he spent off-duty hours acquiring studio expertise and

Above: The line-up that recorded the classic Sailor *LP; from left Lonnie Turner, Boz Scaggs, Tim Davis, Steve Miller and Jim Peterman. Opposite: Miller on stage in the early Seventies.*

committing songs to tape. Then, in September 1966, he moved yet again, this time to San Francisco, where the music scene was about to explode.

Here he formed the first incarnation of the Steve Miller Blues Band, bringing together the talents of drummer Tim Davis – late of Madison band the Chordaires, contemporaries of the Night Train – bassist Lonnie Turner and guitarist James 'Curley' Cooke. While playing at the Matrix Club they attracted the attention of Chet Helms of Family Dog fame: a support gig to Buffalo Springfield followed, they were headlining at Helms' Avalon Ballroom by January 1967 and the next stop was the Fillmore West. Their vinyl debut, a live album backing the notoriously intractable Chuck Berry at that venue, was highly unsatisfactory; September 1967 saw the itinerate Boz Scaggs return from India to join the band in place of Curley Cooke, while bespectacled organist Jim Peterman had also been added before the recording of *Children Of The Future* in early 1968.

Many Bay Area bands had been signed in the wake of June's Monterey Pop Festival and, having learned from his experience with Epic, Miller held out for a better deal than most. 'When I did my contract,' he commented, 'it revolutionised the whole recording industry as far as musicians go ... our contract was five times

better than the Beatles, four times better than the Airplane.' Armed, then, with Capitol Records' reputed 75,000-dollar advance and the artistic freedom to go with it, the band – who had now dropped the 'Blues' from their name – jetted to London to record at Olympic Studios with producer Glyn Johns, whose stock was high from engineering the Beatles' *Sgt Pepper* album the previous year. The partnership paid immediate dividends for, although *Children Of The Future* wasn't in the *Pepper* class, it constituted a promising debut.

Living in the USA

The first side was satisfyingly adventurous, its five segued tracks – all Miller compositions – growing in intensity from the calm that followed the cacophonous opening to 'Children Of The Future'. As if to emphasise the band's common denominator of the blues, the second side saw the mellotron give way to Hammond organ for a mix of Scaggs and Miller originals with a clutch of blues standards, such as 'Key To The Highway'.

The follow-up album, *Sailor* (also produced by Johns in Los Angeles and released in October 1968), has since come to be regarded as one of *the* West Coast albums of the late Sixties era. But the music it contained stubbornly defied description – indeed, its refusal to sustain a mood was aggravating in the extreme with Miller and Scaggs, the principal songwriters, seemingly intent on different courses. The assured tranquillity of Miller's McCartneyesque 'Dear Mary' was shattered by the arrival of Scaggs and Davis' blues-rocker 'Dear Friend', while the sub-Stones riffing of Scaggs' 'Dime-A-Dance Romance' hardly seemed to belong on the same album as Miller's surreal psychedelic instrumental 'Song For Our Ancestors' that had started the same side.

Like so many acts of their era, the Steve Miller Band had trouble in consolidating their initial success – understandably so, since Boz Scaggs had packed his bags for the Atlantic label. Nevertheless, both albums had their moments: *World*'s 'Space Cowboy' was the first of many Miller compositions to venture into the cosmos and was co-written by keyboardist and one-time occasional Night Train member Ben Sidran, whose task it was to replace both Scaggs and Peterman (who had retired to become a producer).

Your Saving Grace's choicest cuts had included the gentle country-rock of the title track and Steve's delicate arrange-

ment of the traditional folk-blues 'Motherless Children' (later to be treated with somewhat less subtlety by Eric Clapton). The trio of Miller, Davis and Turner had been augmented by session pianist Nicky Hopkins, but by the time the scene had shifted to Nashville's Cinderella Sound Studios for the recording of *Number Five* (1970) nothing could be predicted for certain. The departure of Scaggs and Johns had given Miller total control of songwriting, production and performance: using that freedom was to prove a problem.

'Trouble with the engineers' saw Ben Sidran hastily summoned to rescue the project which, although seemingly intended as a further move into country rock, ended up only confused. The sleevenote, dedicating the album variously to NASA, Paul McCartney, Johnny Cash and President Nixon – 'we love you 'cos you need it' –

Steve Miller (above) and his many bands: on stage at Knebworth, 1975 (inset) with Lonnie Turner and Les Dudek, and seven years later in Europe (below).

reflected the record's mix of country, pop, politics and heaven-knows-what. Personnel changed almost daily: session man Bobby Winkelman replaced Lonnie Turner on bass and 12-string, brother Jim guested along with various Nashville musicians and the Steve Miller Band credit on the label now seemed curiously inappropriate.

Eight-track fun
At this point Tim Davis, an inconsistent drummer at the best of times, had bowed out; Miller's comment: 'He's a good singer, a personality, he really fills out the drums – but he can't keep time'. Miller's cohorts for the half live/half studio *Rock Love* (1971), drummer Jack King and bassist Ross Vallory, may have been technically competent, but the results were woefully uninspired.

Steve Miller
Recommended Listening

Sailor (Capitol ST 2984) (Includes: Song For Our Ancestors, Living In The USA, Gangster Of Love, Overdrive); *Fly Like An Eagle* (Mercury 9286177) (Includes: Mercury Blues, The Window, Fly Like An Eagle, Take The Money And Run, Rock'n'Me).

Recall The Beginning ... invited Miller's 1972 offering and, although it failed to match earlier triumphs, it provided a much-needed infusion of new blood in ex-Van Morrison drummer Gary Mallaber, guitarist Jesse Ed Davis, keyboardist Dicky Thompson and the mighty muscular bass of southpaw Gerald Johnson. (Miller had first spotted Johnson backing the Sweet Inspirations vocal group as warmup act for an Elvis Presley show.) The album also had its musical highspots: aided by Ben Sidran's production, 'Enter Maurice' provided Miller with another persona to add to his collection, while 'Journey From Eden' had a certain moody magic that provided hope for the future.

That hope was amply fulfilled by *The Joker*, the LP that finally took Steve Miller from a cult audience to the charts in 1973. Miller's masks on the cover represented some by-now familiar characters and a few new ones: the title track swiftly climbed to the top of the Hot Hundred, its irresistible 'wolf-whistling' slide guitar making it a jukebox favourite. The album contained such further gems as the bass-driven, onomatopoeic 'Shubadadumama' and a tongue-in-cheek cover of the Clovers' 1954 hit 'Your Cash Ain't Nothing But Trash' – performed in true 'Gangster Of Love' style – that saw Miller back in the dock. The album was upbeat, perfect FM radio fare, ideal for the car eight-track and his most commercial offering for years.

Released in 1976, *Fly Like An Eagle* was a product of two months in CBS' old San Francisco studios and Miller was to make his second shot at stardom count. He had met an English girl on his appearance at the 1975 Knebworth Festival and his happier personal circumstances seemed to be reflected in the optimism of the title track and the sentimental ballad reworking of Sam Cooke's 'You Send Me'. The album's other well-known cover was K. C. Douglas' 'Mercury Blues', a number Miller had picked up in his bar-band days and recorded for the *Revolution* film soundtrack around the *Children Of The Future* period. The guitarist had come full circle; with Gary Mallaber reclaiming the drumstool and Lonnie Turner retained on bass, this was Steve Miller's finest hour.

The intelligent use of synthesiser to link the tracks gave the album a unity possessed by few of Miller's earlier releases. Yet the individual songs made strong singles: 'Rock'n'Me' became his second US chart-topper, as well as opening his account in the UK (where Mercury had taken over release of his product) at Number 11. The now-obligatory outlaw rocker, 'Take The Money And Run', scored at Number 11, while the title track of *Eagle* made it a Hot Hundred hat-trick at Number 2.

The *Eagle* sessions had yielded so many songs that 1977's *A Book Of Dreams* was planned around a nucleus of the remainder. Far from being of inferior quality, these songs – 'Jet Airliner' and 'Swingtown' among them – provided the basis for

another rash of singles, making Numbers 8 and 17 respectively in the US charts. Of the other tracks, Les Dudek's 'Sacrifice' stood out with Miller's typical hi-lo double-track vocals and a guitar solo of measured intensity.

With two successive albums of undeniable class, Miller had found the consistency that had eluded him for so many years. But just as a commercial momentum had been established, Miller went to ground – or to be more accurate, to the land. He had become a gentleman farmer and a four-year gap bridged only by two compilation albums was to elapse before his next release – and this disappointed.

Miller goes macho
Rumours that *Circle Of Love* (1981) would be a disco album were only half right: the first side contained four country-flavoured Miller songs harking back to his 1970 recordings, while the second was to split critics and fans alike. 'Macho City' was an 18-minute opus founded on a Gerald Johnson bassline that could well have graced a Bee Gees B-side. The lyrics, an attempted update on 'Living In The USA', threw together Afghanistan, Iran and sundry other hotspots in a transparently facile lyric amid a wash of synths and echoplex guitar. Yet somehow, because it was Steve Miller, it was *almost* audacious enough to cut it. For once, it seemed, the man was letting his reputation do all the work.

The once-divorced Miller's personal life had taken another downturn, it seemed, but drummer Mallaber had not been inactive meanwhile. Having set up his own recording studio, he formed a new band, Kid Lightning, with guitarists and songwriting partners John Massaro and Kenny Lee Lewis. Mallaber sent three songs – 'Young Girl's Heart', 'Something Special' and 'Things I Told You' – to Steve for his comments. Unpredictable as always, he not only liked the songs but added the guitarists to the *Circle* band of Mallaber, Johnson and keyboardist Byron Allred to form a new Steve Miller Band.

1982's *Abracadabra* was a UK Top Five album of original material, but after failing to follow up its success in 1984 with the patchy *Italian X-Rays* the guitarist took solace in the past, featuring the blues of Jimmy Reed on 1986's *Living In The 20th Century* and going one stage further with the Ben Sidran produced jazz covers album *Born 2B Blue* (1988). With someone as unpredictable as Miller, the next move could be in any direction.

No matter what future style he chose, Steve Miller could justifiably claim to bring a sense of humour to adult-orientated rock without selling out totally on his longstanding fans. Few survivors of the late Sixties retain any commercial clout in their second decade. Along with the crew of the Starship, Miller seems to have found a new relevance in the Eighties as well as new worlds to conquer.

MICHAEL HEATLEY

Jeff Beck's wayward talents found many outlets

Rough 'n' Ready

WHEN ERIC CLAPTON left the Yardbirds in 1965, disillusioned with the commercial route they were taking, it seemed unlikely that the group would be able to replace their highly talented guitarist with one of similar merit. But the unknown Jeff Beck was to prove a more than worthy successor, his distinctive style and imaginative use of feedback and other revolutionary effects establishing him rapidly as a guitar hero in his own right.

Strident Tridents

Beck was born near Richmond, Surrey, in 1944 and became interested in music at an early age. 'My mother used to force me to play piano about two hours a day,' he recalled years later. 'But that was good because it made me realise that I was musically sound. My other training consisted of stretching rubber bands over tobacco cans and making horrible noises.' Beck soon graduated from tins to a real guitar – 'a beaten-up old acoustic thing. It had one string but that's all I needed. One string was plenty for me to grapple with.' When this broke, he improvised by building another out of a cigar box, but this second instrument soon went the way of the first: 'My old man threw it out in the garden because I had a row with him. He busted it,' said Beck.

After leaving school, Beck studied at Wimbledon Art College ('I used to go there because they had good meals,' he recalled) but dropped out in 1963 to take up the guitar full-time. By now, Beck had acquired a cheap electric instrument along with a love of the blues: 'My interest in blues started when the Chicago blues albums began to reach England. I grabbed them – Muddy Waters, Buddy Guy – I thought they were great. There's a special way the guitars sound – sort of tinny and rough.' By 1964, Beck had joined struggling London R&B band the Tridents and was playing in clubs such as Eel Pie Island and the 100 Club for £5 a night.

When Clapton quit the Yardbirds shortly after recording Graham Gouldman's 'For Your Love', the group invited session man Jimmy Page to take his place. Page turned down the offer, but suggested they check out the Tridents' guitarist. One night, after a Tridents gig, Giorgio Gomelsky, manager of the Yardbirds, did so, as Beck later recalled: 'After the set we

talked about a job he had for me with a new group and I said "No. Go away you nasty little man."' Beck quickly changed his tune, however – after all, the Yardbirds had just been in the Top Ten.

Right from the start, Beck stamped his individual style on the music of the Yardbirds. Much less of a blues purist than Clapton, Beck wanted to experiment with different forms, integrating sustain and feedback into his playing: 'My amp was always whistling so I'd kick it and bash it and it would feed back. I decided to use it rather than fight it. The ideal thing was to get the beauty of the feedback – *controllable* feedback.'

Beck's chosen guitar was a Fender Esquire that he had bought for £30 from John Maus of the Walker Brothers; the sounds he coaxed from the instrument during his 18-month stint with the Yardbirds were remarkable, from the abrasively psychedelic solo on 'Shapes Of Things' to the sitar-like patterns of 'Over Under Sideways Down', from the rapid-fire repeats and humorous fills of 'Nazz Are Blue' (from the 1966 album *Yardbirds*) to the strident rhythms and wailing police-car effects of 'Happenings Ten Years Time Ago'. It was Beck, too, who began to introduce auto-destructive elements to the Yardbirds' live act. 'When I joined the Yardbirds, I got the impression they just wanted my playing to enhance their group as much as possible,' he has said. 'So I just worked on the whole act until we got it down so great that we started bringing in bits of destruction to illustrate a point. Like an action painting – we all sort of threw our guitars at it.'

But while Beck's equipment-smashing antics were, like those of the Who's Pete Townshend, sometimes contrived, they were more often born out of frustration: 'The amp would be crackling or my guitar would be out of tune or Keith Relf would be coughing and spluttering on stage. There's nothing more frustrating than going on with so much to say and not being able to put it out so I used to give angry little jabs at the speaker and if it went up in a cloud of smoke then I was happy. But if it just stayed there stubbornly and was still crackling, I'd give it some stick.'

Beck's erratic behaviour and uneven temperament swiftly led to friction within the Yardbirds. From the beginning he had felt musically frustrated: 'I was restricted so badly that I used to be like a naughty boy and play weird things all the time,' he recalled. When Beck withdrew from an

American tour in October 1966, leaving Jimmy Page to cope with all guitar duties, the group decided to dispense with Beck's services. He turned his energy towards forming a band of his own, a band that would give him more space in which to manoeuvre.

The silver lining

Columbia Records, the Yardbirds' label, offered him a deal in which Mickie Most was assigned to production. Beck assembled the talents of ex-Shadows bassist Jet Harris and ex-Pretty Things drummer Viv Prince, adding a second guitarist in Ron Wood (whom Beck had known since 1964 when the Tridents had often supported Wood's R&B group, the

Insets opposite: The Yardbirds with Beck, 1966 (centre); Beck's 1968 band (bottom), from left Mickey Waller, Beck, Rod Stewart and Ron Wood; and the Jeff Beck Group of the early Seventies (top). Right: Beck and Gibson Les Paul.

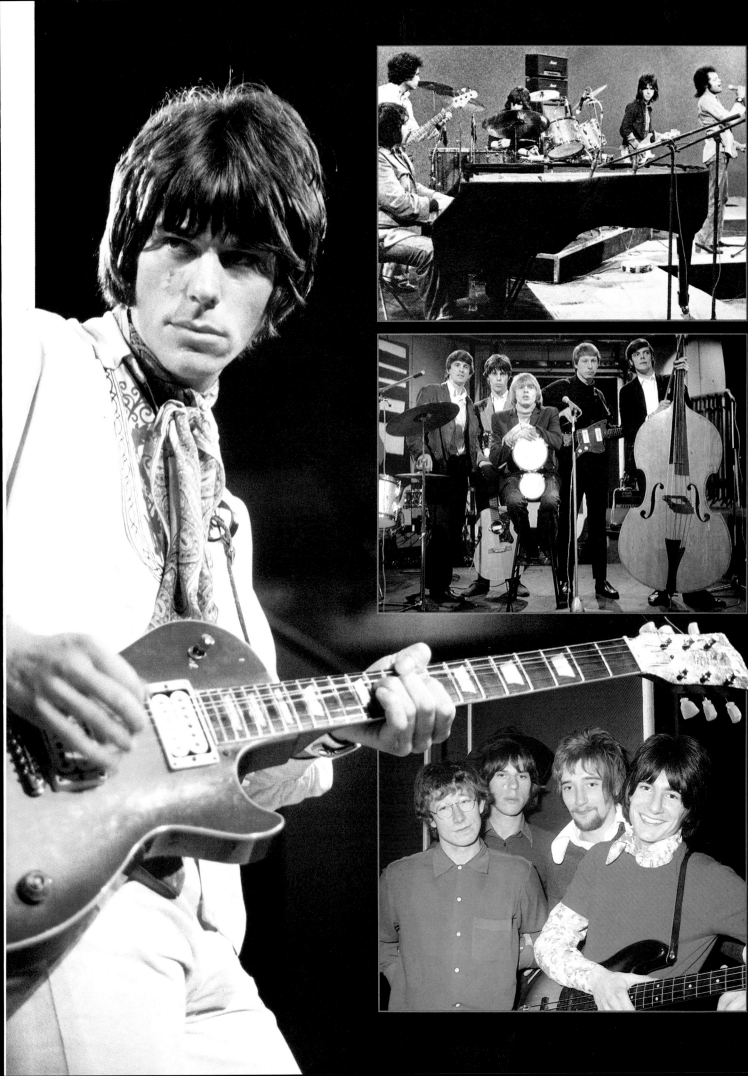

Birds). This unlikely aggregation failed to make it past the rehearsal stage, however; Prince and the unreliable Harris were dismissed, Prince being replaced by ex-Tridents drummer Ray Cooke and, still lacking a bass player, the group were taken into the studio by Most to record a single.

'Hi-Ho Silver Lining', a catchy, commercial number with an infectious dance-hall beat, was quite out of keeping with Beck's intentions for a 'progressive' hard rock, guitar-based band and his workmanlike, unadventurous solo seemed to reflect his irritation at Most's designs on the pop charts. Arranged by John Paul Jones (soon to join Led Zeppelin) who also contributed bass, the record climbed the UK charts, peaking at Number 14 in April 1967.

By this time a new bass player had been found in Dave Ambrose of the Brian Auger Trinity and a vocalist, Rod Stewart (ex-Steampacket and Shotgun Express), was added in time to sing on the B-side of Jeff Beck's second single. The A-side, 'Tallyman', was a fine song written by Graham Gouldman (who had been responsible for several Yardbirds numbers) and contained a scintillating, swerving and sweeping slide guitar solo from Beck. The record made Number 30 in the UK charts in August, but the band still seemed unable to stabilise its line-up. Cooke departed to be replaced by a succession of drummers – Rod Coombes, Aynsley Dunbar (formerly with John Mayall's Bluesbreakers) and, finally, Mickey Waller. Dave Ambrose, meanwhile, had been sacked because of his failure to attend rehearsals, Ron Wood switching from guitar at the end of 1967 to replace him.

Cosa Nostra Beck-Ola

Truth, which emerged early in 1968, was dominated throughout by Beck's endlessly inventive and creative guitar work, from the opening cut – a re-arranged, louder and harder version of 'Shapes Of Things' – to the closing track, Willie Dixon's 'I Ain't Superstitious', which Beck confessed in the liner notes was 'more or less an excuse for being flash on guitar'. From the crude and raucous work on another Dixon number, 'You Shook Me' ('Last note of song is my guitar being sick,' wrote Beck), through the restraint of Tim Rose and Bonnie Dobson's 'Morning Dew', to the lyrical playing on 'Beck's Bolero' (written by old Yardbird colleague Jimmy Page for the B-side of 'Hi-Ho Silver Lining'), Beck's guitar made *Truth* a classic of late-Sixties British hard rock. And while Mickie Most was still trying to turn Jeff Beck into a pop commodity ('Love Is Blue', a dreadful version of Paul Mauriat's equally appalling orchestral hit, scraped into the Top Thirty in March), the steady sales of the album – which eventually made the LP Top Twenty – indicated that the group's future lay more with the 'progressive' audience.

Top left: Beck, Bogert and Appice. Top right and right: Jeff Beck on stage.

But although the band meshed together as well on stage as on record, providing the ideal backdrop for Beck's wizardry, the group's personal relationships were less satisfactory. Stewart, whose gritty and grating delivery added much to the overall sound, felt left out of the limelight, while Beck felt that Waller and Wood were failing to provide adequate rhythmical backing. During an American tour in early 1969, Beck decided to fire the rhythm section; as Stewart later recalled: 'He sacked Ronnie and Mickey then he got Tony Newman on drums and an incredibly bad Australian bass player [Junior Woods] who rehearsed with us once, the night before we went on stage. That was in Washington DC and we died the all-time death. So the bass player got sent back to Australia and Jeff called back Ronnie Wood. By that time Ronnie was really fed up.'

Nonetheless, the second LP, *Beck-Ola*, released in the spring of 1969, was another extraordinarily well-executed hard rock album. Beck delved further into his seemingly bottomless bag of tricks to snatch out the startling staccato slide interlude on Elvis Presley's 'All Shook Up' – a song transposed from rock'n'roll to heavy metal without resorting to cliché – while the staggering pyrotechnics on 'Plynth (Water Down The Drain)' and the shift between rage and sensitivity on the instrumental *tour de force* 'Rice Pudding' provided further highlights.

Too much aggravation
The album was a commercial success and, following a Most-instigated collaboration with Donovan on the single 'Barabajagal', the Jeff Beck Group set off on another American tour which was supposed to culminate in an appearance at Woodstock. But Beck's crew was not to be a part of the 'half-a-million strong' to grace Max Yasgur's pastures that August, for before the festival had got under way the guitarist's temperamental behaviour had finally proved too much for Wood and Stewart – the group was no more. 'I couldn't take all the aggravation and unfriendliness that developed,' said Stewart in 1974. 'It was getting too ridiculous for words near the end. In the two years I was with Beck, I never looked him in the eye – I always looked at his shirt or something like that.'

While Wood and Stewart went off to team up with ex-Small Faces Ronnie Lane, Ian McLagan and Kenney Jones in the Faces, Beck made plans to form a power trio with drummer Carmine Appice and bassist Tim Bogert, once the rhythm section of Vanilla Fudge who had so impressed him when he saw them in 1967. But before this project could get off the ground, Beck had crashed his sports car and been severely injured. By the time he had fully recovered, some 18 months later, Appice and Bogert were otherwise engaged with a new band, Cactus. Beck countered by putting together a new group of his own with fellow hot-rod car fanatic Cozy Powell (drums), Max Middleton (piano), Clive Chaman (bass) and Bob Tench (vocals).

The Jeff Beck Group recorded two albums for Beck's new label Epic, the first of which, *Rough And Ready* (1971), was yet another showcase for Beck's endless innovation. The guitarist's sidemen – and, in particular, powerhouse drummer Powell – complemented him perfectly to produce an extended essay in intelligent heavy metal. Although the second LP, *Jeff Beck Group* (1972), boasted excellent performances all round, it was desperately short of substantial material; for the first time, Beck's admitted inability to write songs was proving a problem.

Pomp and virtuosity
In June 1972, Bogert and Appice both left Cactus and Beck was finally able to join forces with the rhythm section he so admired. His admiration proved short-lived, however, for Beck, Bogert and Appice turned out to be an egocentric power trio, full of pomp and virtuosity, signifying nothing. The band recorded an eponymous debut album, released in 1973, and found a particularly appreciative audience in Japan, but Beck himself loathed the project: 'Beck, Bogert and Appice were uncreative and self-indulgent,' he was to admit. 'They thrived on excess and overplaying. If you could zero in on the energy, you got the goods, otherwise it was a cacophonous, horrible noise. I was doing a bottle of Smirnoff a day just to survive it all.' One more Beck confession summed up the root of the trio's problem, and it was a problem that would haunt the guitarist in years to come. It was simply this: 'We were grappling with an abysmal lack of material.'

Beck spent the months following the group's demise in 1974 revaluating his musical ideas; he began to feel that he had accomplished all he could within the field of hard rock and found his tastes leaning more and more towards jazz and funk music. Deciding to explore a form of music that 'crosses the gap between white rock and Mahavishnu or jazz-rock', he went to AIR Studios to record a new album under the production auspices of George Martin.

Blow By Blow (1975) turned out to be an uneven collection of instrumentals that ranged from a jazzy cover of the Beatles' 'She's A Woman', through aimless funk workouts to misconceived catastrophes like 'Diamond Dust', which was soaked in unnecessary Martin orchestration. The performances of the guitarist's chosen backing musicians were professional at best and the material itself was, again, uninspiring. Beck's subsequent recordings – *Wired* (1976) and *There And Back* (1980) – and his 1976 collaboration with the Jan Hammer Group, which afforded the LP *Jeff Beck With The Jan Hammer Group Live* (1977), showed that his great instrumental abilities were still intact but were

all, still, marked by a distinct lack of excitement.

Beck remains an honest musician, however; he acknowledges his shortcomings as a composer, continues to seek out material that best suits his needs and admits that this search is often fruitless. He is determined to move on and, unlike so many of his contemporaries and disciples, is never content to rest on his laurels.

He cut an uninspiring LP *Flash* (1985) which reunited him with Rod Stewart, attempted an unlikely recording alliance with punk Svengali Malcolm McLaren and guested on Mick Jagger's solo albums.

Although Beck continued his quest for originality in the Eighties, his real achievements lay back in the Sixties. With the Yardbirds, his search for new sounds bridged the gap between R&B and art-pop/psychedelia, while he later helped to sow the seeds of British hard rock and heavy metal with his own group. Only Jimi Hendrix and Eric Clapton can rival the invention and the influence of Jeff Beck.

TOM HIBBERT

Above: Jeff Beck relaxes in the dressing room with Fender, cheroot and fellow guitar hero Eric Clapton. Both were formerly members of the Yardbirds. Below: Beck tramps the streets, axe at the ready.

JEFF BECK
Discography to 1980

Singles
Hi-Ho Silver Lining/Beck's Bolero (Columbia DB 8151, 1967); Tallyman/Rock My Plimsoul (Columbia DB 8227, 1967); Love Is Blue/I've Been Drinking (Columbia DB 8359, 1968); Got The Feeling/Situation (Epic 7720, 1972); Black Cat Moan/Livin' Alone (Epic 1251, 1973); She's A Woman/It Doesn't Really Matter (Epic 3334, 1975); The Final Peace/Space Boogie (Epic 8806, 1980).

Albums
Truth (Columbia SCX 6293, 1968); *Beck-Ola* (Columbia SCX 6351, 1969); *Rough And Ready* (Epic EPC 64619, 1971); *Jeff Beck Group* (EPC 64899, 1972); *Beck Bogert & Appice* (Epic EPC 65455, 1973); *Blow By Blow* (Epic 69117, 1975); *Wired* (Epic EPC 86012, 1976); *Jeff Beck With The Jan Hammer Group – Live* (Epic EPC 86025, 1977); *There And Back* (Epic EPC 83288, 1980).

STILL ALIVE AND WELL

Johnny Winter twangs his thang and hollers the blues. In his early work, the wiry albino guitarist created an exciting mixture of traditional blues and high-energy rock.

A FRAGILE, WEAK-SIGHTED albino guitarist who sings the blues with a raucous black holler, Johnny Winter must be one of the least likely performers to have emerged from America's Deep South. He was born on 23 February 1944 in Leland, Mississippi, and grew up in Beaumont, Texas. His father played banjo and sax and sang in church choirs, while his mother played piano; in this musical environment Johnny and his younger brother Edgar (also albino) quickly learned to play several instruments. Johnny began on clarinet at five years of age, then took up the ukelele and guitar.

Winter began listening to the blues when he was about 11. 'I hadn't heard anything like it before,' he later admitted. 'I just bought everything I could find.' With pocket money earned from mowing lawns and clearing rubbish, he built up a large collection of records, buying from mail-order record shops that sponsored R&B radio shows; he particularly admired Howlin' Wolf, Muddy Waters and Lightnin' Hopkins. Later the reissued recordings of Robert Johnson would also appeal to Winter.

In 1959, at the age of 15, Winter made his recording debut at Bill Hall's Beaumont Studio. This record, 'Schoolday Blues', by Johnny and the Jammers, was leased to Houston's Dart label the following year. Brother Edgar played piano on this rock'n'roll dance tune, while Johnny played lead guitar and sang in the smoky voice that characterised so many East Texas and South Louisiana artists. 'It sold 285 copies and got to Number 8 in Beaumont,' said Johnny. After leaving high school and then dropping out of business college, he headed north to Chicago where he hung around on the fringe of the blues scene there, watching artists like Muddy Waters and sitting in on jam sessions.

The early Sixties also saw Winter playing with local bands Gene Terry and the Downbeats, with his brother Edgar in It and Them (which later became the Black Plague) and with Roy Head's group, the Traits. As well as doing numerous sessions with other artists, Winter cut a number of singles on regional labels, and Houston producer Roy C. Ames leased a 22-track session of downhome country blues to the Atlantic label in 1967.

'I recorded just about every kind of thing imaginable,' said Winter, 'as well as a little blues, there was a Louisiana influence, some hillbilly, rock'n'roll and cajun-type stuff.' Many of Winter's early recordings were re-released once he had become an international star (these included the albums *First Winter, About Blues* and *Early Times*). In fact his official debut album *Johnny Winter* (1969) was pre-empted by an unofficial release a few months earlier – *The Progressive Blues Experiment*, a rather grandiose title for a local label recording intended as a glorified demo to hawk around the major companies. In a review in *Rolling Stone*, however, Pete Welding suggested the official debut album did not have the looseness, excitement, intensity or urgency of Winter's earlier work.

Freak show

Winter's first mention in *Rolling Stone* was in 1968 – the year that he formed a trio with Tommy Shannon on bass and John Turner on drums – when Larry Sepulvado, in a feature on music in Texas, tipped him as 'the hottest item outside of Janis Joplin ... a hundred and thirty pound cross-eyed albino with long fleecy hair playing some of the gutsiest fluid blues guitar you have ever heard.' East Coast club owner and entrepreneur Steve Paul read the review and, in the words of critic Lillian Roxon, he 'snapped like a divining rod that had at last stumbled onto water.' Paul flew to Houston, heard Winter and signed him to a management contract, after which he brought Winter to New York and set him to work at his

Scene Club. Winter's popularity swiftly escalated, and in December 1968 he secured a booking at the prestigious Fillmore East where he provoked a tremendous response.

Steve Paul, now in a strong bargaining position, secured Winter a 600,000-dollar recording contract in 1969 with Columbia Records. The media was quick to latch onto the guitarist's strange looks and presence in a predominantly black blues scene, and he received a lot of publicity that tended to bracket him with the likes of Tiny Tim (also managed by Steve Paul). Such publicity sold records, however; *The Progressive Blues Experiment* reached the Top Fifty while *Johnny Winter* made Number 24.

Though this 'freak' status undoubtedly helped in attracting initial attention, Johnny Winter's appeal ran much deeper. On both his debut album, and especially the follow-up LP, *Second Winter* (1970), he achieved a subtle synthesis of traditional blues and the high-energy, high-noise electric guitar pyrotechnics initiated by Hendrix. *Second Winter* was recorded in Nashville in late 1969 and featured John Turner on drums, Tommy Shannon on bass and brother Edgar on sax and keyboards.

Hang on Johnny
The 1971 album, *Johnny Winter And*, signalled a movement away from his blues roots towards a more progressive, acid-rock feel. He was joined by three ex-members of the McCoys, a group from Indiana who had enjoyed a worldwide hit with 'Hang On Sloopy' in 1965 – Randy Hobbs (bass), Randy Z (drums) and Rick Derringer (guitar and vocals). Randy and Rick were brothers, formerly sharing the surname Zehringer. Rick was a talented guitarist and singer, and Winter utilised him to the full as part of a dual instrumental and vocal attack.

Johnny Winter has always been primarily a stage performer, and the Johnny Winter And group was probably his best line-up. On stage, Derringer assumed the role of MC, exhorting the crowd between numbers to clap, shout louder or whatever, while Winter would totter around in the background, making occasional forays towards the microphone to yell 'rock'n'roooll' at the top of his voice. But it was always Winter's show: even when Derringer was singing, it was hard to look away from the lanky, white-haired figure with the crazy eyes and wild grin playing outer-space blues with deceptive ease. With Randy Z having been replaced by Bobby Caldwell on drums, the 1971 live album, *Johnny Winter And Live*, which included many classic performances, notably 'Good Morning Little Schoolgirl', 'Johnny B. Goode', and the Rolling Stones' 'Jumpin' Jack Flash', was Winter's most successful album in Britain.

Winter, now at the height of his popularity, was also heavily involved with drugs and in a desperately weak physical condition. He went into semi-retirement,

Above: Winter with Rick Derringer, who joined him in 1971. Below: Winter jams with Muddy Waters (centre) and James Cotton.

spending a year in River Oaks Hospital, New Orleans, emerging in 1973 with a new band and an album aptly entitled *Still Alive And Well*. Winter was indeed glad to be alive, and the album reflected this exuberance. On the title track he sang in wry tones: 'Did you ever take a look to see who's left around?/Everyone I thought was cool is six feet underground.' Elsewhere on the album he delved into country with 'Ain't Nothing To Me', old-time Delta blues on 'Too Much Seconal' and confirmed his position as prime Jagger-Richards interpreter with strong versions of 'Silver Train' and 'Let It Bleed'.

Since the mid Seventies Winter has been active as a producer for Steve Paul's Blue Sky record label. It was here that he came to provide inspiration for his old hero Muddy Waters – the man who had himself been an early inspiration to Winter.

Waters' career had been in decline but Winter produced and played on his 1977 album *Hard Again*, and subsequently toured as part of Waters' band.

Throughout the Seventies Winter continued to release albums that generally contained a mixture of blues standards, originals and covers. *John Dawson Winter III* and *Saints And Sinners* (both 1974), *Captured Live* and *With Edgar Winter: Together* (both 1976), and *Nothin' But The Blues* (1977) were by no means bad records, but they lacked the fiery genius of much of his earlier work and sounded dated. Winter became the victim of culture lag; cut off from the Sixties spirit of musical adventure and operating in an area increasingly dominated by heavy metal bands, he lost his constituency. He visited Britain in May 1979 to promote his *White Hot And Blue* album released the previous year, and with Jon Paris (bass/harmonica) and the outstanding Bobby Torello on drums, he released *Raisin' Cain* in 1980.

By 1985 he'd moved to the US blues label Alligator, for whom he opened his account with *Serious Business*.

DAVID SINCLAIR

Johnny Winter
Recommended Listening

Johnny Winter And (CBS 64117) (Includes: No Time To Live, Prodigal Son, Nothing Left, Rock'n'Roll Hoochie Koo, Let The Music Play); *Johnny Winter And Live* (CBS 64289) (Includes: Good Morning Little Schoolgirl, Jumpin' Jack Flash, Johnny B. Goode, Rock'n'Roll Medley: Great Balls Of Fire/Long Tall Sally/Whole Lotta Shakin' Goin' On).

TAJ MAHAL

Natural blues and international rhythms

LIKE LEADBELLY before him, Taj Mahal has annexed much of America's musical heritage and carried it into the present. Unlike Leadbelly, however, Mahal's vision of America stretches out to the Caribbean, the Latin republics and includes tenuous links with an African ancestral home. It is no accident that around 1959 the singer – originally named Henry Fredericks – settled on the name Taj Mahal, a fitting assertion of Third World loyalties.

Mahal/Fredericks was born on 17 May 1942 in New York and was raised in Springfield, Massachusetts. His mother came originally from Cheraw, South Carolina, where she counted Dizzy Gillespie among her childhood acquaintances. In 1934 she moved to New York where she met her husband, a West Indian who earned his living as a jazz arranger. Her own preference ran to gospel and classical song so, not surprisingly, the Fredericks inadvertently sowed the seeds of their son's musical diversity.

A Rising Son

After a period at college studying animal husbandry and singing downhome blues and raw soul in his spare time, Mahal embarked on his professional career with the Rising Sons, a folk-rock outfit working the Los Angeles area in the mid Sixties. The Rising Sons – who also included future Byrd Kevin Kelley and guitarists Ry Cooder and Jesse Ed Davis in their line-up – were signed to Columbia Records but after just one single, 'Candy Man'/'The Devil's Got My Woman' (1966), the label dropped them; a completed album was never released.

Nonetheless, the company were sufficiently impressed with Mahal's talents to sign him as a solo act and in 1967 released his debut LP, *Taj Mahal*. Backing was provided by Davis and Cooder with Gary Gilmore on bass and Charles Blackwell on drums. 'The group mirrored exactly what I thought,' Mahal has since asserted – and certainly they caught the mood of the time in a tight, hard-driving electric blues set which still succeeded in honouring authentic country roots. Material by Ma Rainey, Robert Johnson and Sonny Boy Williamson rubbed shoulders with three Sleepy John Estes compositions, including a superb update of his 'Diving Duck Blues'.

The album's finest moment was a reading of Blind Willie McTell's 'Statesboro' Blues' where Mahal infused an antique song with entirely contemporary urgency. The same change overtook Johnson's 'Dust My Broom', a blues classic from the mid Thirties reinterpreted in the manner of Elmore James. The album was a remarkable debut, a testament to Mahal's fabled eclectic powers and a celebration of classic American music. As Mahal exuberantly remarked, 'I got more good heroes than Wild Bill Hickok had notches on his belt!'

The Natch'l Blues in 1968 sensibly worked the same ground with outstanding performances in 'Good Morning Miss Brown', 'I Ain't Gonna Let Nobody Steal My Jelly Roll' and 'The Cuckoo', but most significant was the inclusion of 'You Don't Miss Your Water', a soul ballad in the classic Memphis tradition. First recorded by William Bell on Stax in 1961, it was successfully revamped by Otis Redding in 1966. Mahal's impassioned vocal, supported by the Stax-Volt stylings of a horn section comprising Plas Johnson, Jim Horn and J. J. Johnson, also impressed.

Opposite: Taj Mahal, vintage 1968. Above: An early Mahal group line up with Jesse Ed Davis (second from left).

Evidently Mahal was a singer, guitarist and harp player who could step beyond the blues, and the double album *Giant Step/De Ole Folks At Home* (1969) confirmed this view. On the first record, Mahal presented his electric music; alongside material from Leadbelly and the like was the unabashed pop of Goffin and King's 'Take A Giant Step' (originally recorded by the Monkees). In marked contrast was the grim gospel of Blind Willie Johnson's 'You're Gonna Need Somebody On Your Bond', ideally suited to Mahal's graveyard delivery, which vied for attention with a charging version of 'Six Days On The Road'.

Rags and roots

The second record featured Mahal accompanying himself on acoustic renditions of long-forgotten rags, worksongs and blues. It did not matter that contemporary black audiences knew little and cared less about men like Leadbelly, Henry Thomas or the Reverend Gary Davis. Mahal was restating the neglected Southern country roots of black America. He was speaking to spirits and settling accounts. The closing song, 'Annie's Lover', was liable to slip past those radical militants who had nodded off. In devoting it to an African man, a natural man, Mahal was depicting himself and talking roots long before it became fashionable.

In 1971 'West Indian Revelation', from *Happy Just To Be Like I Am*, took up the torch with Mahal describing himself as 'First, a black African; second, a black Jamaican; third, a black American!' New recruit Kwasi Dzidzorhu from Ghana supplied the percussion, while Andy Narell played steel drums.

The same year Mahal began a final foray into exclusively American music with *Recycling The Blues And Other Related Stuff*, completing the project in 1973 with *Ooh So Good'n'Blues*. Finely calculated contributions from the Pointer Sisters and tuba player Howard Johnson helped reconcile primitive blues moaning to the sophisticated gloss of the big band era. On the first set Mahal managed to include his flamenco instrumental 'Gitano Negro', the glittering first fruit of a six-month sojourn in Spain. On his next album, *Music Keeps Me Together* (1975), the Third World princeling was revelling confidently in calypso, cajun and reggae.

Tickled in Trinidad

In cinematic circles Mahal's skill had been recognised as early as 1972 when he scored Martin Ritt's film, *Sounder*. He followed this by writing the music for 'Almos' A Man', a TV film based on a story by Richard Wright. In 1976 he found time to guest on Bonnie Raitt's *Takin' My Time* before firing his parting shot for the Columbia label with the warmly accomplished funk of *Satisfied'n'Tickled Too*.

That same year Mahal switched to Warner Brothers, cut an undistinguished soundtrack in *Brothers*, then turned his attention back to transglobal black culture. *Music Fuh Ya* was one of the delights of 1977, with songs ranging from Elizabeth Cotten's 'Freight Train' to the calypso beat of 'The Four Mills Brothers'. The mainstay of Mahal's International Rhythm Band was steel drummer Robert Greenidge from Laventille in Trinidad. He helped transform the blues into carnival, as several cuts on *Evolution: The Most Recent* demonstrated during 1978. 'Salsa De Laventille', an instrumental penned by Greenidge for that set, summed up the state of fusion music under the aegis of Taj Mahal.

In 1979, Mahal devoted himself to direct-cut recording on his live performances, perhaps mindful that his artistry is such that it has never received full justice under studio conditions; the results, *Taj Mahal And International Rhythm Band*, were issued on the Crystal Clear label that year.

Mahal has never been a clinical archivist like Bonnie Raitt or Ry Cooder; every song has been an attempt to tell people about the world he lives in.

After an eight-year break, Taj Mahal returned to recording in 1987 with *Taj*, but its easygoing Afro-Caribbean sound—influenced by his Hawaiian surroundings—was a far cry from the innovation of old.

CLIVE ANDERSON

Taj Mahal
Recommended Listening

Giant Step/De Ole Folks At Home (CBS 866226) (Includes: Take A Giant Step, Six Days On The Road, You're Gonna Need Somebody On Your Bond, Annie's Lover, Bacon Fat, Stagger Lee).

BLUES IN BLOOM

Mike Bloomfield: from sideman to solo star

A PIONEER OF ELECTRIC blues guitar, Mike Bloomfield perfected a style that assures him a place in rock history. His tragic death in 1981 went almost unnoticed, and yet this was the man *Rolling Stone* magazine once hailed as a leading light of 'the new electric music'.

Born in Chicago in 1943, Michael Bloomfield was the only son of wealthy Jewish parents. At the University of Chicago, he struck up a friendship with Nick Gravenites, who was helping to organise the university's annual Folklore Festival, a showcase for bluegrass instrumentalists and country blues singers through to gospel quartets. Bloomfield was soon captivated by the poetic qualities of country blues legends such as blind Tennessee singer-guitarist Sleepy John Estes and Mississippi slide guitarist Big Joe Williams, and took up playing acoustic guitar himself, also studying blues piano alongside Gravenites.

In 1963, Bloomfield made his recording debut, playing second guitar on a couple of tracks by Sleepy John Estes for the specialist blues label Delmark. Soon after this, blues harmonica player Charlie Musselwhite blew into town, recruiting Bloomfield and Gravenites into a regular working unit to accompany visiting bluesmen. John Hammond Sr, Columbia Records A&R chief, heard a demo tape of the band and signed them to a one-off album deal, which unfortunately fell through. By now, Bloomfield had switched to electric guitar, jamming regularly in South Side blues clubs with the likes of Muddy Waters, Buddy Guy, Otis Rush and Albert King. Early rock'n'roll guitar styles also fascinated him, in particular those of Presley's guitarist Scotty Moore and Cliff Gallup, lead guitarist with Gene Vincent's Blue Caps.

Butter and jam
About the same time, Paul Butterfield was attracting local attention with his strikingly authoritative approach to the blues. His amplified harmonica work was excep-

Below: The Butterfield Blues Band in 1966 with Mike Bloomfield (second from left). Above: Al Kooper (right) with Paul Simon.

tional, steeped in jazz phrasing in much the same manner as that of his mentor, Little Walter Jacobs. His regular band at this time featured Tulsa-born Elvin Bishop on lead guitar and local keyboardist Mark Naftalin, plus two former sidemen from Howlin' Wolf's band – bassist Jerome Arnold and drummer Sam Lay. Jac Holzman, boss of Elektra Records, flew in from Los Angeles to check them out, immediately signing them to an album deal with options. 'Butterfield came over to see me,' Bloomfield reminisced. 'Said he wanted a slide player to sit in on the album sessions.'

Bloomfield took most of the lead guitar passages, and also wrote or co-wrote three of the songs, while his friend Nick Gravenites contributed the opening track, 'Born In Chicago'. Suddenly the Paul Butterfield Blues Band were the talk of the town. Bloomfield's guitar with its dynamic attack, natural sustain and savoury vibrato was charged with tension, complementing Butterfield's expressive, heavily amplified harmonica. Chuck Berry was impressed enough with the duo to invite them to his *Fresh Berry's* album sessions at the local Chess studios. They featured on the opening track, 'It Wasn't Me'.

Hitting the highway
Some weeks later, Bloomfield received a telephone call from Bob Dylan, whom he had met at a party in Chicago, inviting him to participate in the *Highway 61 Revisited* recordings in New York where Bloomfield met organist Al Kooper. Kooper recalled the date in his book *Backstage Passes*: 'Suddenly Dylan exploded through the doorway, and in tow was this bizarre-looking guy carrying a Fender Telecaster guitar *without* a case. It was the dead of winter and the guitar was all wet from the rain and the snow. He just shuffled into the corner, wiped it off, plugged it in and commenced to play some of the most incredible guitar I ever heard.'

Late in 1965, the Butterfield Blues Band entered Elektra's studios to record the monumental *East-West*, the focal point of which was the 13-minute title track, written by keyboardist Naftalin and Gravenites. An awesome instrumental built on an ascending raga scale, it displayed the solo talents of Bloomfield, Butterfield and Bishop to the full. A revelation at the time, it set the scene for numerous 'jams' in the latter half of the Sixties. 'It was the best band I'd ever been in,' Bloomfield said later. 'Elvin wanted to play lead guitar again, so I went off to form the Electric Flag.'

Regarded as something of a supergroup, the Flag brought together a bunch of musicians who'd been around for several years but had never played together as a unit. Drummer Buddy Miles was recruited from Otis Redding's band, while other members included Harvey Brooks (bass), Barry Goldberg (organ), a four-piece horn section and Nick Gravenites on rhythm guitar and vocals. Bloomfield dubbed them 'An

Above: Bloomfield on stage. Above right: Paul Butterfield, supremely gifted blues harp player. Below: Bloomfield (right) in the studio with Bob Dylan.

American Music Band' after they made their debut at the 1967 Monterey Pop Festival. The group sound veered more towards hard rock than the Chicago blues Bloomfield had been playing with Butterfield, spurred on by Miles' relentless drumming. Their debut album, *A Long Time Comin'*, released by Columbia in early 1968, was a subtle mix of R&B and soul, featuring original numbers interspersed with a few blues classics.

Film producer Roger Corman heard the album and hired the group to score the music for his psychedelic movie, *The Trip*. Because of its controversial nature, the film received a complete UK ban at the time of its release, and the soundtrack album (on Capitol Records), also failed to get a UK release, even though it featured Bloomfield at the peak of his creativity. The 7 minute 25 second self-penned instrumental, 'Fine Jung Thing', certainly deserved a wider hearing; Bloomfield's fierce lead guitar playing is as representative here as anything he ever committed to record, while the Flag as a group never sounded hotter. The sessions, however,

1239

were marred by several confrontations between Miles and Bloomfield; one final fight ended with Bloomfield quitting the group, which cut one last album before Miles himself left to form the Buddy Miles Express.

By this stage, Bloomfield had moved from Chicago to San Francisco, where he ran into Al Kooper who was on his way to a session with West Coast psychedelic band Moby Grape and invited Bloomfield along. The end result was captured on the Grape's second album *Wow/Grape Jam* (1968) – an improvised set from Kooper and Bloomfield that was to inspire them to record the *Super Session* album.

Born in New York City in 1944, Kooper had been playing in chart bands since the late Fifties, had written a hit – 'I Must Be Seeing Things' – for Gene Pitney, and had helped form the Blues Project with Danny Kalb, Steve Katz, Tommy Flanders and Artie Traum. He went on to form Blood Sweat and Tears, leaving soon after to go solo. He was to play on three Bob Dylan albums, later working with Jimi Hendrix and the Rolling Stones.

The 1968 *Super Session* was his first major solo assignment, for which he was joined by Bloomfield and Stephen Stills, who was then between Buffalo Springfield and Crosby, Stills and Nash. The line-up was completed by Harvey Brooks (bass) and Eddie Hoh (drums). The record was acclaimed by musicians and fans alike, and remained in the charts until late 1969. The next couple of years were especially active for Bloomfield: he guested on Janis Joplin's *I Got Dem Ol' Kozmic Blues Again Mama*, cut an album (*Two Jews' Blues*) with Barry Goldberg, released a solo LP *It's Not Killing Me* and appeared on *Live At Bill Graham's Fillmore West*.

He also found time to record a live double-album with Al Kooper, *The Live Adventures Of Al Kooper And Mike Bloomfield*. Although the critics panned it as 'self-indulgent', it provided a fitting close to the musical excesses of the late Sixties, and gave Bloomfield his last chart success.

The bloom fades
Bloomfield's career then went into a sharp decline. He began to experiment with heroin, and later became involved in two projects that were doomed to failure. The first was an ill-matched liaison with Dr John and John Hammond Jr for the album *Triumvirate*, released by Columbia in 1973. He tried again with another 'supergroup', KGB, comprising Ray Kennedy, Rick Grech, Barry Goldberg and Carmine Appice. Their debut LP on MCA sold half a million copies, but Bloomfield disowned it: 'It was a pre-programmed mould,' he later confessed. 'They recorded it in LA, then flew the tapes to San Francisco; I just overdubbed my parts.'

As the Seventies progressed, Bloomfield became more and more interested in writing film scores. His works included *Medium Cool* (photographed by his cousin Haskell Wexler) and Andy Warhol's *Bad*. For the movie soundtrack to *Steelyard*

Top: Paul Butterfield jams with Maria Muldaur. Above: Though better known as a keyboard player, Al Kooper is equally at home on guitar. Along with Bloomfield and Butterfield, Kooper made a great contribution to white electric blues.

Blues, he was reunited with Paul Butterfield and Nick Gravenites, but the music was fairly uninspired.

Although Bloomfield had become something of a recluse by the mid Seventies, the public still remembered him. In 1976 he was named Best Electric Blues Guitarist in the *Guitar Player* magazine readers' poll, topping the acoustic section two years later. By way of thanks, Bloomfield recorded a special album, *If You Love These Blues, Play 'Em As You Feel*. Financed by the magazine, it conveyed Bloomfield's own feelings towards the idiom, as he narrated and demonstrated various acoustic and electric guitar styles.

By the latter half of the Seventies, Bloomfield had carved a niche for himself that he at last seemed happy with: a recording contract with specialist label Takoma alongside the occasional solo gig in the Bay Area. The intense, screaming guitar solos that were so much his trademark in the Sixties were now replaced by acoustic music filled with rare poetic quality. Albums like *Analine* and the *Bloomfield/Woody Harris* collaboration display this very different side to the guitarist, the latter comprised solely of guitar duets, on a selection of spirituals including 'Peace In The Valley' and 'Just A Closer Walk With Thee'.

Bloomfield's last recording, *Cruisin' For A Bruisin'*, was released late in 1980 and coincided with the guitarist making a short solo tour of folk clubs and coffee houses, playing a mixture of traditional songs and show tunes like Sophie Tucker's 'Some Of These Days'. In addition to guitar, Bloomfield also played five-string banjo and accordion.

The last hours in Bloomfield's life are still shrouded in mystery. He was found dead in the passenger seat of his beige 1971 Mercury, parked in the Forest Hills area of San Francisco on Sunday morning, 15 February 1981, with an empty bottle of Valium on the adjacent seat. The official verdict was death by a drug overdose. The previous evening, however, Bloomfield had attended a fashionable music business party, and it's rumoured that he had OD'd in the early hours of the morning and that his body had been driven to Forest Hills to avert any publicity.

His final concert appearance, just a few weeks before his death, was with Bob Dylan, who called him onstage at San Francisco's Warfield Theatre. Bloomfield plugged in his Stratocaster for a rousing 'Like A Rolling Stone', leaving the stage to a standing ovation. It was probably the way he'd most like to be remembered.

DAVE WALTERS

The Festive Generation

Rock music and the sound of the crowd

To SOME PEOPLE, the rock festivals of the late Sixties and early Seventies represent one of the peaks of rock's achievement in creating a generation with a new awareness. But to their critics, these festivals show how the 'rock generation' could take itself too seriously, and could force a vital music along paths that led to its ossification.

Summer holidays

The festivals mark an eight-year period of rock's history. They were well under way by 1969, when the greatest of them all, Woodstock, took place; and by 1977, when a new wind was blowing, the spirit that had animated them was gone. But what was the essential spirit that lay behind the festival years? Whatever it was, it was not – in spite of frequent assertions – merely the spirit of flower power and hippiedom; for by the time the festivals were really taking off, flower power was already a thing of the past. It is undeniable, however, that ideas of peace and love were an important part of the whole phenomenon. Rather, perhaps, festivals should be seen as one of the examples of rock being subsumed into middle-class culture. They were the pastime of a generation that was keenly interested in rock; these people had considerable spending power, were able to take unlimited time off at certain times of the year and were old enough not to be classed as runaways if they stayed away from home for several days.

The audience that fulfilled all these norms was the late-teenage/early-twenties school and college-going public. And they were essentially middle-class, or about to move into the middle classes when they graduated. That is not to say that no-one else went to festivals; but that the critical element lay in this part of the audience.

These schoolchildren and students (or dropped-out students) were not just going to hear the music; that merely gave them an aim. They were going for something to do while on holiday, and chose to go to festivals for the same reason that their parents went on holiday to certain places – to be with other members of their own kind in an atmosphere in which they could relax and enjoy themselves. Actual appreciation of the music or the artists would be difficult because of frequently poor sound systems and their distance from the stage; and the physical conditions – bad toilets, lack of food and cover – were frequently appalling.

Naturally, the next generation of rock fans, in a more cynical and economically depressed world, reacted against this; and so the festival ideal died. But not before it had been responsible for some of the great moments in rock's history.   ASHLEY BROWN

In 1970 hordes of fans descended on the sleepy Isle of Wight to see and hear Jimi Hendrix.

FESTIVALS DIARY

1965

25-27 July Newport Folk Festival, Rhode Island, USA Bob Dylan horrifies the folk purist sections of the audience by playing an electric rock set; backing is provided by the Paul Butterfield Blues band featuring Mike Bloomfield and Al Kooper.

8 August National Jazz and Blues Festival, Richmond, UK Alongside jazzers, the cast list includes the Rolling Stones, the Yardbirds, Manfred Mann, the Spencer Davis Group and Steampacket; the day culminates in an on-stage jam featuring Chas Chandler of the Animals, Gary Farr, Long John Baldry, Rod Stewart and Steve Winwood.

1966

1 August National Jazz and Blues Festival, Windsor, UK The Who's destructive stage act gets out of hand when sections of the audience decide to join in by smashing chairs and ripping tent canvas.

1967

14 January The First Human Be-In, Golden Gate Park, San Francisco, USA Thousands of hippies, and many local groups, gather to celebrate the Summer of Love.

16-18 June Monterey Pop Festival, California, USA An enormous turnout and an impressive roster of talent emphasise rock's new maturity; performances by the Jimi Hendrix Experience, the Who, Otis Redding, Jefferson Airplane, Big Brother and the Holding Company, Country Joe and the Fish and others are filmed for a movie of the event.

26-28 August Festival of the Flower Children, Woburn Abbey, UK Among the acts at this commercially-oriented event are such non-flower-power outfits as the Alan Price Set, Marmalade and the

Bee Gees; other delights include free flowers, sparklers and a firework display every night. The Duchess of Bedford, whose husband owns Woburn Abbey, appears somewhat bemused by it all, telling *The People* newspaper: 'I thought it was going to be a flower show with competitions, prizes and lots of flowers.'

1968

13-16 June Third International Festival of Pop Songs, Bratislava, Czechoslovakia Acts include Cliff Richard, Gene Pitney and the Easybeats.

21 June Midsummer Night's Dream Festival, Burton Constable, Hull, UK An array of 'progressive' acts turn out, including Family, Elmer Gantry's Velvet Opera, Spooky Tooth and the Savoy

Below left: The Duke of Bedford, owner of Woburn Abbey, inspects hippies on his lawn at the Festival of the Flower Children, 1967. Below: The programme for 1969's Isle of Wight Festival. Bottom: The Rick Griffin-designed Human Be-In poster, 1967. Below right: The Grateful Dead play a marathon set at 1970's Hollywood Music Festival.

Brown Blues Band, while the crowds afford pop chart act Marmalade a less than generous reception.

1969

The big festival comes of age with enormous gatherings at Atlanta, Denver, San Fernando and Woodstock in US and on the Isle of Wight, UK.

5 July Hyde Park, London, UK 'Wow, some people guess the crowd's reached over half a million,' said compère Sam Cutler as the masses poured into the park to see the Rolling Stones. 'I hope those of you who can't see the bandstand heard that.' Other acts to grace that bandstand on the day included King Crimson, the Screw, Family and the Battered Ornaments.

3-6 July Newport Jazz Festival, Rhode Island, USA The festival's first ever major rock presentation included Led Zeppelin, Ten Years After, Jeff Beck, Jethro Tull and James Brown.

15-17 August Woodstock Music and Arts Fair, New York State, USA Jimi Hendrix, the Who, Creedence Clearwater Revival, Crosby, Stills and Nash, the Band, Jefferson Airplane, Sha Na Na, Joe Cocker, Janis Joplin, Joan Baez and others, along with 400,000 spectators, help give birth to the 'Woodstock Generation' down on Max Yasgur's farm.

31 August Isle of Wight Pop Festival, UK Bill is topped by a scoop appearance by Bob Dylan and the Band which causes more rock giants to be sitting in the audience than there are on the bill.

31 September Toronto Peace Festival, Ontario, Canada John Lennon and the Plastic Ono Band perform along with rock'n'roll legends Little Richard, Chuck Berry, Bo Diddley and Gene Vincent.

6 December Altamont, California, USA The free festival spirit of the

Rolling Stones concert is destroyed when spectator Meredith Hunter is stabbed to death by Hell's Angels.

1970
23 May Three rival UK festivals are held on the same day:
Bath City Pop Festival A modest crowd gather to listen to Quintessence, Wildmouth, Wishbone Ash, Argent, Fleetwood Mac, Juicy Lucy, Sam Apple Pie and others.
Plumpton Pop Festival This two-day event kicks off with performances by Tom Rush, Warm Dust, May Blitz, Audience, Van der Graaf Generator and Free.
Hollywood Music Festival, Newcastle-under-Lyme Highlight of the day's proceedings (which includes performances by Family, Radha Krishna Temple, Steppenwolf and Demon Fuzz) is an appearance by newcomers Mungo Jerry, while the event is headed by the Grateful Dead, who play for four hours.
3-5 July Atlanta Pop Festival, Georgia, USA Features Captain Beefheart, Jimi Hendrix, Ginger Baker's Airforce, the Allman Brothers Band and others.
26 August Isle of Wight Pop Festival, UK Atrocious sound quality, rain and violence mar the event for the vast majority of the 200,000 present; Jimi Hendrix plays in the UK for the last time.

1971
20 June Glastonbury Fayre, Wiltshire, UK Britain's remaining hippies gather to celebrate the summer solstice; highlight of the festival is an appearance by David Bowie.

1972
1-3 April Mar Y Sol Festival, Puerto Rico Features performances by Emerson Lake and Palmer, J Geils Band, Mahavishnu Orchestra, the Allman Brothers Band, Dr John and others.

30-31 May Great Western Express Festival, Bardney, Lincolnshire, UK 40,000 people witness Roxy Music's first major performance.
8 September Ann Arbor Jazz and Blues Festival, USA In memory of Otis Spann, the event features Muddy Waters, Howlin' Wolf, Freddie King, Junior Walker and other bluesmen.

1973
28 July Summer Jam Festival, Watkins Glen, New York State, USA The largest festival crowd to date – some 600,000 – watch the Band, the Grateful Dead and the Allman Brothers Band.

1975
5 July Knebworth Festival, Herts, UK 100,000 view the spectacular effects

Above left: Supersession at Richmond, 1965. From left Chas Chandler, Gary Farr, Rod Stewart, Long John Baldry and Steve Winwood. Above: Paul Simenon of the Clash (left) and the Police's Sting relax between sets at the early punk festival at Mont de Marsan, 1977. Left: Bob Dylan serenades 200,000 of his British disciples at Blackbushe Airfield, 1978.

of Pink Floyd; the Steve Miller Band and Captain Beefheart also put in appearances.

1976
Mont de Marsan, France The first European punk rock festival; bill includes the Damned, Nick Lowe, Eddie and the Hot Rods, the Tyla Gang, the Count Bishops and those stalwarts of free festivals of an earlier age, the Pink Fairies.

1977
Mont de Marsan, France The second European punk rock festival; the Clash play, along with many of the previous year's participants. The Jam, dismayed by conditions, refuse to perform and return home.

1978
15 July Blackbushe Airfield, Surrey Bob Dylan tops a bill that includes Eric Clapton, Graham Parker and Joan Armatrading; attendance estimated at 200,000.

1980
Monsters of Rock, Donington, UK The first of an annual series of concerts for heavy metal groups is headlined by Rainbow. In subsequent years, acts of the stature of Bon Jovi (1987) and Iron Maiden (1988) headline, but the latter event is blighted by the deaths of two youths allegedly from the effects of 'slam-dancing'.
DAFYDD REES

BAREFOOT IN THE PARK

UK festivals from Beaulieu to Knebworth

THE RIOTS THAT INTERRUPTED the Beaulieu Jazz Festival in 1960 confirmed the prejudices of most postwar parents about young people and the strange music they listened to. Television cameras, there to capture a weekend's jazz, instead transmitted pictures of chairs being smashed, scaffolding collapsing and teenagers climbing onto the stage, pulling musicians' instruments from their mouths and ripping their clothes.

The Jazz Festival had attracted a strangely diverse crowd ever since it started in 1955. Many sessions were punctuated by jeers and boos as opposing camps of modern and trad jazz fans heckled each other's heroes. Yet, at the same time, courting couples innocently jived in the surrounding parkland and Sunday morning open-air Church services, led by Johnny Dankworth, Cleo Laine and a guitar-strumming monk called Brother William, were always well attended. But a second bout of trouble in 1961, despite barbed wire and the presence of 64 policemen, persuaded Lord Montagu of Beaulieu – in whose grounds the event was held – to abandon it forever.

Nonetheless, jazz and folk festivals flourished throughout the Sixties. In August 1961, the first National Jazz Festival took place at Richmond in Surrey with top British names like Chris Barber and

Above: The Beaulieu Jazz Festival offered a taste of things to come in the shape of annual riots. Left: The Stones play Hyde Park. Below: Their audience get playful. Top left: By the time Hyde Park played host to Queen in 1978, however, these free concerts had become something of a ritual, lacking the spontaneity of the originals.

Dick Charlesworth playing alongside a number of lesser-known provincial bands. Later changing its name to the National Jazz and Blues Festival and moving to Windsor and then Kempton, this was to become the biggest regular music event of the decade. Partly as a result of the CND movement, folk made great strides, too, and *Melody Maker* greeted the birth of the Keele Folk Festival in 1965 with the headline: 'At Last, A British Newport!' By 1967, there were 10 regular jazz and folk festivals a year in the UK.

1967 was also the year, however, when John Lennon infuriated many jazz fans by announcing that both mainstream jazz and

Dixieland 'are dying, man – like the Black and White Minstrels'. And indeed, rock and pop music had by now made sufficient inroads into these festivals to warrant events of their own. Cream, for instance, gave their first major performance at the sixth National Jazz and Blues Festival in July 1966; the following year saw jazz relegated to Saturday afternoon to make room for artists like Jimi Hendrix, the Kinks and the Small Faces.

It was this tradition of jazz and blues festivals that produced the first significant event devoted almost entirely to rock music – at Woburn Abbey, country home of the Duke of Bedford, in July 1968. Partly organised and promoted by *Melody Maker*, it presented Fleetwood Mac, Taste, Al Stewart, Tim Rose and Donovan, among others.

But the enormous gatherings of the late Sixties and early Seventies didn't just develop out of the earlier festivals. They came also from a sense that an alternative society was evolving and a feeling that

music might change the world: ideas that, in 1968, were being forged in London in a small corner of Hyde Park near the Serpentine where, one balmy Saturday afternoon in June, about 2,000 people – all slightly amazed that they didn't have to pay – sat on the grass to watch Pink Floyd, Jethro Tull, Tyrannosaurus Rex and Roy Harper. Disc jockey John Peel called it an event 'which carried with it more love and more hope than I believed possible'. A few weeks later everyone was back at the same venue to see the Nice, Traffic and the Pretty Things.

There were three Hyde Park concerts altogether that summer and more the next. They quickly established a routine: the chances of the Edgar Broughton Band appearing, to chant 'Out, Demons, Out!', were always pretty high, and the Third Ear Band were often there too. Donovan would also sometimes turn up uninvited and parody himself ('Yellow is the colour of my true love's teeth – in the morning . . .') during interminable *ad hoc* stage acts which he – at least – seemed to enjoy immensely.

The free concerts, organised by Blackhill Enterprises, were part of a much wider London scene that genuinely believed this new music was in the vanguard of inevit-

The second Isle of Wight Festival, 1969. Some fans found they could actually see and hear Bob Dylan better from outside the festival area (opposite), while some climbed on friendly shoulders (below). Still more were content to just take the day as it came, play with foam (inset left) or paint their faces (inset below left).

able political change: at venues such as Middle Earth in Covent Garden and the Roundhouse people came to celebrate and share ideas as well as dig the music.

The Rolling Stones ruined all that – although no one quite realised it at the time – by playing a free Hyde Park gig in June 1969 in front of half a million people. Free concerts were now for everyone and in the years and events that followed – Blind Faith, Free, Jack Bruce – the intimacy and shared ideals that had motivated them originally were easily lost in the crowd.

At the same time, these ideas were being squeezed by commercial interests which, especially after Woodstock, saw the chance of a quick financial killing. This often led to a clash between the expectations of the promoter – easy money – and those of the audience, who were frequently encouraged to believe that they were spending a few days in some kind of alternative society.

At the 1970 Isle of Wight Festival, for instance – the year after Bob Dylan's performance there – the stadium was cramped, the sound appalling, the performers often not in view and the sanitary facilities disgraceful. Many fans escaped to the hillside overlooking the arena, where the events were visible for nothing, the sound happened to be perfect and the atmosphere more in line with what they'd been led to expect.

Even the performers were unhappy – 'Give me some respect . . . I'm an artist' screamed Joni Mitchell as the audience talked through her act and threw drink cans at the stage when she outstayed her welcome. And the event ended in chaos with thousands leaving early, hoping to

miss the rush off the island, and a contingent of French anarchists wreaking havoc. 'Why are you doing this to us?' compère Ricki Farr pleaded from the stage. 'We've given you this festival in peace and love and you're breaking down our shops. You've broken down our fences.'

By the following year there were festivals all over the place – Lincoln Racecourse, Essex University, Clitheroe in Lancashire (although Glasgow's Festival of a Thousand Heads had to be called off in the face of local opposition) and, just occasionally, this uneasy alliance between promoters and punters paid off. In fact, if ever there was a typical (and successful) pop festival, it was Weeley in 1971 – even down to the terrified inhabitants of the local village (population 1,000) who spent all summer hoping it wouldn't actually happen. There were the typical messages over the PA system, the typically never-ending programme – T. Rex, the Faces, King Crimson, Mott the Hoople, Stone the Crows, Vinegar Joe and a cast of thousands – and the typically abandoned timetable, with almost continuous music from Friday to dawn on Monday.

Despite this being the summer of 'Maggie May', Rod Stewart and the Faces played second to T. Rex and Marc Bolan, now a teenybop idol, was obviously nervous appearing in front of an older, more critical audience: 'Hi, I'm Marc Bolan. You've probably seen me on "Top of the Pops",' he joked. Everyone booed. Run for charity by Clacton Round Table, Weeley was one of the last big festivals to have a wholly pleasant atmosphere.

For most of the Seventies, the festival scene was dominated by the annual events of Knebworth and Reading. Both were huge affairs that lacked any consistent identity, and there were constant complaints from support acts having to play at half-volume so that top-of-the-bill bands would sound more impressive. Knebworth, in particular, went for big-name groups – 200,000 saw the Rolling Stones play in 1976 – while Reading 1980 must at least be short-listed for the title of worst British festival ever, as 30,000 heavy-metal fans got drunk, hurled cans, headbanged and played imaginary guitars in fields thick with mud and rain.

By then, Dylan had already provided a brief reminder of earlier days, when, at Blackbushe Airfield near Camberley in Surrey in 1978, and sporting a crumpled top hat, he whipped through a short set of radical re-arrangements of well-known favourites. One-time hippies travelled from all over the UK and, as the concert ended, thousands of cars – where once there would have been rucksacked hitchhikers – blocked each other's paths in a gigantic traffic jam that took until the middle of the next morning to clear.

Meanwhile, the hundred-odd people making their own music on the edge of the festival played happily on, as they'd done through Dylan's act. These were the remainder of a dedicated number who had

spent the Seventies trying to keep the idea of free music alive. The Festivals of the People they had held during the early Seventies in Windsor Great Park – too near the Castle for the High Court's liking – attracted persistent police attention. In 1974, in scenes of violence that far exceeded those at Beaulieu 14 years before, 600 police broke up the festival after those attending refused to leave. Poet Heathcote Williams later sued the local commissioner for loss of faith in the police; not surprisingly, he lost.

More commercial attempts to resurrect the past, such as Glastonbury Fayre in 1981 with its crafts and theatre workshops, have been little more than embarrassing; and interesting attempts to break new ground – like the 1982 WOMAD festival at Bath that featured an exciting range of ethnic music but failed to balance the books – seem unable to engage enough popular support really to take off as annual events. Jazz and folk festivals, on the other hand, have typically been smaller and left to their own devices, and have survived

Above: Knebworth, where Led Zeppelin provided the headlining attraction in 1979. Below: A fan struts his funky stuff to Hawkwind at Richmond.

more or less intact. Regular events in the late Seventies included the Newcastle Jazz Festival and Crewe Folk Festival, while London's Capital Radio entered the market with an annual jazz weekend. The Cambridge Folk Festival entered the Eighties as the largest UK event of its type, but its diversification into less folky territory in terms of acts billed has threatened to compromise its previously exemplary atmosphere.

All through the Seventies, however, pop festivals were resisted and cancelled or went ahead and flopped. Increasingly, government regulations made them seem less exciting and they were soon, in all but name, simply open-air concerts. There was little sense of shared identity and there was nothing much to celebrate. By the mid Seventies the dreams of the Woodstock generation had died.   COLIN SHEARMAN

WOODSTOCK

'Let me take you higher,' sang Sly and the Family Stone (below). Sure enough, the assembled 500,000 at Woodstock got higher, even if they had to climb the scaffolding

Peace, love and a movie moneyspinner

THE CELEBRATION that took place on Max Yasgur's farm near Bethel in upstate New York over the weekend of August 15, 16 and 17 1969 represented the spirit of the decade probably better than any other single event in the Sixties. On closer examination, 'Woodstock Nation' proves to be as ephemeral and insubstantial as one would expect from a weekend gathering of hippies, even if it briefly transformed the sleepy hamlet of Bethel into the third largest city in New York State. But as a symbol of the contradictory and confused hopes the burgeoning counter-culture brought forth from the underground ghettoes of San Francisco and London, Woodstock reigns supreme.

Unlimited capital

The festival, its gates long since trampled down and any attempt to charge admission given up, began at 5.00 on the Friday afternoon when Richie Havens ambled to the stage to perform for the 200,000 strong crowd. It came to life an hour later when Country Joe McDonald chanted his own special version of the 'Fish Cheer'—'Give

me an "F", five me an "I", give me a "S", give me an "H". What's that spell?' It ended at 9.30 am on the following Monday when Jimi Hendrix played 'Purple Haze' to the 30,000 who stayed on until the very

last. In between, the attendance briefly touched the half-million mark and, in conditions that veered from balmy sunshine to torrential rain, the festival-goers survived the failure of essential sanitary services and the lack of food (both a regular feature of festivals) and still maintained an atmosphere that for the most part was indeed characterised by 'peace and love'.

The festival – or the 'Woodstock Music and Arts Fair: an Aquarian Exposition', to give it its full title – grew directly out of a meeting on 6 February between John Roberts, Joel Rosenman, Artie Kornfeld and Michael Lang. Roberts and Rosenman were Ivy League graduates who had turned their backs on law and Wall Street respectively for careers as would-be television writers. They hit on the idea of having a couple of trouble-shooter financiers as the linch-pin of a TV series, but then couldn't think of ideas for their fictional duo to explore. To find odd projects they placed an ad in the *Wall Street Journal* with the intention of borrowing the ideas presented to them and no more: 'Young Men with Unlimited Capital looking for interesting, legitimate, investment opportunities and business propositions.'

Most of the ideas they received were ridiculous, but a few were intriguing

Above: Director Mike Wadleigh won the 1970 Oscar for Best Feature Length Documentary for his film Woodstock. *Below: Joe Cocker gave a characteristically sweaty performance. Above right: David Crosby (left) and Graham Nash later sang the theme song for Wadleigh's film with CSN&Y.*

enough to make them quit their prospective careers as TV writers to try out the role of financiers; in this they were greatly aided by Roberts' family fortune which meant that they really could invest in unusual projects. One of the first such ventures they attempted was Media Sounds, a new recording studio complex in New York. It was an immediate success and brought Challenge International to the attention of Lang and Kornfeld, who were promoting a studio complex in the Woodstock area. Lang, who would quickly become the guiding force of the festival, was a street hustler who had made it to the fringes of the music business when he had persuaded Kornfeld, Capitol's head of East Coast A&R, to sign Train, a band that Lang managed.

Festive fun

Lang and Kornfeld's first meeting with Rosenman and Roberts was unfruitful, but at the next one Lang suggested an open-air concert to publicise the studio, mindful of the stars like Bob Dylan and the Band who lived in the vicinity. And so was born the Woodstock Festival – out of the desire of Lang and Kornfeld to make their mark in the rock business and of Rosenman and Roberts to put on the largest festival ever.

Lang would always remain the prime mover, the man whose energy and boundless enthusiasm for the project in the early months kept it alive. But if Lang was the moving force, as the festival lurched closer and closer to actuality it seemed as if it was being willed into being by the people it was put on for. As Roberts' resources were stretched to the limit and the original half-million dollar budget was exceeded (any prospect of a profit disappearing with it), only the immensity of the project kept it alive.

What everyone thought was going to be the hardest problem, getting performers, was easily overcome in a manner that suggested how each subsequent problem could be solved – overpayment. Creedence Clearwater Revival were the first to sign up on 10 April when they agreed to play for the (then) grossly inflated sum of 10,000 dollars. With a major band on the books and big money in the offing, an impressive roster was quickly assembled; the week beginning 21 April alone saw the signing of Canned Heat (13,000 dollars), Johnny Winter (7,500 dollars) and Janis Joplin (15,000 dollars). Dealing with the underground politicos wasn't quite as easy. Eventually, at a meeting of students and radicals, it was voted that the festival be a weekend of fun rather than a political event, much to the relief of Roberts and Rosenman – but not before Abbie Hoffman, leader of the extreme-left Yippies organisation, had demanded and obtained 10,000 dollars (in small bills, of course) after threatening to denounce the festival as a 'capitalist rip-off'. The organisers paid up because their investment was so great and their fear of losing 'street credibility' – and thus an audience – was equally great.

Down the Alley

However, the major problem was obtaining a suitably large site. That seemed solved when Howard Mills agreed to lease land and the town council of Wallkill agreed to host the festival after being misled by Lang as to its size and character. But as the preparations got underway and the inhabitants of Wallkill began to realise the true nature of the plans, a rising tide of animosity against hippies finally resulted in a new town ordinance that made it impossible to hold the festival there. With 31 days to go, the gates of Wallkill had been padlocked against peace and love. (Woodstock had its revenge on Mills and Jack

Woodstock: The Performers
Joan Baez
The Band
Blood, Sweat and Tears
The Butterfield Blues Band
Canned Heat
Joe Cocker
Country Joe and the Fish
Creedence Clearwater Revival
Crosby, Stills and Nash
The Grateful Dead
Arlo Guthrie
Tim Hardin
The Keef Hartley Band
Richie Havens
Jimi Hendrix
The Incredible String Band
Jefferson Airplane
Janis Joplin
The Joshua Light Show
Melanie
Quill
Santana
John Sebastian
Sha Na Na
Ravi Shankar
Sly and the Family Stone
Bert Sommer
Sweetwater
Ten Years After
The Who

Schloser, Wallkill's town supervisor who had led the anti-festival fight: Arnold Skolnick's poster to publicise the change of venue featured two stereotype hillbilly characters who bore an uncanny resemblance to Mills and Schloser.)

The festival was rescued by Max Yasgur, who a week later, over several gallons of chocolate milk (his favourite tipple), negotiated himself a tidy sum for the use of his farm and a place in rock history. The festival had a new home and, with the assistance of some two hundred assorted hippies, the real preparations began in earnest. By now the profit motive had fallen by the wayside of Happy Avenue (the aptly-named road that led to the festival). Thus, on the advice of Wes Pomeroy – a policeman in charge of security, who was keen to try passive policing with smiles replacing guns – the planned fence along the festival perimeter was not erected; in its place was a string of youngsters asking people to pay to get in. Similarly, although hamburgers and such were available from the ill-named Food For Love (the company that won the food concession), an alternative company – the Hog Farmers – were also flown in to produce more appropriate counter-cultural fare. The result, as one New York dietician put it, was 'enough macrobiotic food to wipe out the entire US Olympic team'.

Now unstoppable, the festival took on a life of its own as its dimensions began to be appreciated by the likes of the telephone company, sanitary engineers and the Highway Patrol, who had previously turned a deaf ear to appeals for help. One by one the remaining wrinkles were ironed out, with money – as ever – smoothing the way. All that remained was for the audience to trek to Bethel and the performers to be flown in by helicopter. A few problems would occur: the burning of the Food For Love stands, a near-electrical failure, the demand of the Who (and, uncharacteristically, the Grateful Dead) for cash in hand before they would play, and three deaths among the audience. But despite the fears of those who importuned Governor Rockefeller to declare the festival a disaster area, it was Max Yasgur who was proved right. On stage he enthusiastically delivered his verdict on the weekend's events: 'This is the largest group of people ever to have assembled in one place . . . I think you people have proven something to the world – that a half a million kids can get together and have fun and music and nothing but fun and music. And I God bless you for it!'

Standing by Dope Alley (where the dealers congregated) and listening to the big numbers being discussed, the hordes must have found Yasgur's comments naive; by the free stage where the likes of Joan Baez had been regular performers, his remarks seemed commonplace. But then, as the film *Woodstock* demonstrates, Woodstock was all things to all comers, a glorious bash on the world's village green and hippiedom's greatest hour. PHIL HARDY

At their height, rock festivals provided a brief taste of an alternative society. Countless young people set off, packs on their backs, for a few days of utopia (below).

THE NEW UTOPIA

The impossible dream of America's youth

FESTIVALS WERE by no means new to the American music scene when rock music discovered the concept in 1967. Regularly staged and well-organised open-air festivals, lasting from one to several days, had long been a part of the jazz and folk worlds – notably in the form of the Newport Jazz and Folk festivals, held at Newport, Rhode Island, on the US East Coast. The annual jazz festival, in particular, was generous in its interpretation of its title, with blues artists appearing regularly alongside jazz acts. Muddy Waters' Newport appearance was recorded for a superb live album in 1960, while the 1958 festival featured Chuck Berry, who was immortalised on film in Bert Stern's excellent movie documentary of the event, *Jazz On A Summer's Day*.

The rock festival, however, did not arrive on the American scene until 1967, when the Monterey International Pop Festival was brought to fruition by John Phillips, leader of the Mamas and the Papas, entrepreneur Lou Adler and singer Paul Simon. Their concept was of a gathering where artists and musicians of any kind could play their music – free if possible – to a large audience in an atmosphere of peace, love and friendship. In the mood of prevailing optimism, nowhere stronger than on America's West Coast, such a dream seemed within reach.

Because of the pervading good-time mood of the era, the festival concept seemed attractive to many artists and groups, particularly those who were finding themselves grouped, by accident or design, under the umbrella of progressive or underground music. Acts who might not have considered playing such an event in hard-headed financial terms agreed to take part. This attitude prevailed throughout the high days of the American festival era; the events had a sense of identity, purpose, even history about them, which transcended – for a while – the monetary considerations of the performers. Realistically, there is no doubt that such an atti-

Top: Poster for the 1972 Ann Arbor Jazz and Blues Festival, held in memory of blues pianist Otis Spann. Above: David Crosby, Michelle Phillips and Scott McKenzie organise a phenomenon in the Monterey Pop office. Above right: Alvin Lee of Ten Years After keeps his clothes on at Newport, 1969 – but this wasn't always the case.

tude was often exploited to the hilt by festival promoters who mouthed the hippie ideal in public while clutching the fat bankroll tightly behind their backs. But Monterey itself obviously pre-dated such bandwagon profiteering.

Music for the people
Once the success of Monterey had set the ball rolling, there seemed no stopping it. The many similar festivals promoted in the wake of Monterey were no longer regarded as 'pop' festivals but as rock events; Monterey and the progressive music revolution that supported it were instrumental in driving a wedge between the basic, undemanding pop music which fed Top Forty radio and the more committed forms of rock of which commerciality was not the obvious hallmark.

Some 30 rock festivals of varying sizes and kinds were held over the next three years. Some were pure idealistic celebrations of hippiedom; artists performed free for non-paying crowds in virtually nonorganised environments where people were vulnerable not only to heat, rain and mud, but also a near-total absence of sanitary facilities and even food. By way of compensation, some of the on-stage events had their unique features; Ten Years After reported having performed totally nude at a California hippie festival where most of the acts and almost the entire audience had opted for a similar form of communion with nature.

The year of the festival was undoubtedly 1969; Bob Dylan and the Band were lured to Britain to top the bill at the Isle of Wight Festival at the end of August, while back in the USA large-scale events were staged throughout the summer. The Newport Jazz Festival went 'rock' with a vengeance, including acts like Frank Zappa and the Mothers Of Invention, Ten Years After and Jethro Tull, as well as blues and soul outfits like John Mayall's Bluesbreakers, B. B. King, O. C. Smith and James Brown. The same thing happened at the Baltimore and Philadelphia Jazz Festivals shortly afterwards, with British rockers Led Zeppelin, Jeff Beck and Ten Years After among the jazzers. These events all took place during July, as did the huge Atlanta rock gathering with a lengthy bill which included Creedence Clearwater Revival, Chuck Berry, Johnny Winter and Blood, Sweat and Tears. A month earlier, the Denver Pop Festival had also featured Creedence and Winter, along with Joe Cocker, Crosby, Stills and Nash and the Jimi Hendrix Experience. It was August 1969, however, which was to see the year's biggest event, probably the all-time archetype of the outdoor music festival – Woodstock.

Festivals continued apace after Woodstock, many of them openly trying to be equally successful carbon copies. However,

1253

Woodstock's free, spontaneous spirit never arose again in the same way, although (or maybe because) it was constantly being evoked. As late as 1973, the festival at Watkins Glen, New York State, finally broke Woodstock's attendance figures when some 600,000 people spent a day watching the Band, the Grateful Dead and the Allman Brothers Band. It was a beneficiary – in common with all big outdoor and stadium musical events of the Seventies and Eighties – of the sound technology developed at the earlier festivals to enable vast crowds to hear the music. It did not, however, recapture the time-capsule euphoria of its predecessors.

A much more ominous aftermath was the visually documented murder of a member of the audience at Altamont, which stamped an image of savage menace over the environment that Monterey had created in blissful goodwill and optimism. Very much a product of the Sixties, the American festival age passed appropriately on with its decade. BARRY LAZELL

Two camps: 1980's Philadelphia Folk Festival (right) retained a rustic, anti-commercial mood, while the American Rock Technology Festival, held in California in 1982 (below), was an unashamed celebration of consumerism.

Confessions of a Festival-Goer

The 1970 Bath Festival: a personal view

THE BATH FESTIVAL of Blues and Progressive Music, held on Saturday 26 and Sunday 27 June 1970, wasn't in Bath at all. It was in Shepton Mallet – a good 15 miles from the city – and I suppose we should have taken a map because we got hopelessly lost trying to track down the village. Not that it made all that much difference, however, for when we *did* hit the right road, it was jam-packed with vehicles in a similar dilapidated condition to our own, and the traffic was progressing at a considerably slower

Left: Led Zeppelin on stage at Shepton Mallet, Sunday 27 June 1970. Below: The camp site goes on forever – some 300,000 people turned up for the weekend.

rate than the thousands of rucksacked pedestrians trudging indefatigably toward the site in sandals and filthy, patched jeans.

At last we heard the strains of 'progressive' music wafting through the morning's warm air and knew we must be close. At this point – as if signalling a (not unwarranted) dislike of the Keef Hartley Band – the car spluttered and died. We got out and pushed; the trundling hordes ignored our plight.

Hot dog horror

Two-and-a-half miles later we parked, pitched tent, stowed a gallon of best Somerset cider plus other assorted provisions (beans, nasty-looking tins of Irish stew, cheese and onion-flavoured crisps, chocolate digestives) beneath the sleeping bags and wandered down to the playing fields. At the gates, burly figures with armbands saying 'Steward' stood beside a large, ominous sign saying 'Beware of Adders. If bitten . . .'. We queued up with our tickets (£2.10s for the weekend). The queue did not move. At the front, a long-haired youth in a tie-dye shirt held the hand of a very-pregnant girl in grimy paisley smock and pebble specs. The youth was involved in a lengthy discussion with the stewards: 'Look, man, me and my chick have hitched all the way from Northampton 'cause we thought this was, you know, like a *free* festival, not a rip-off festival, and we've got no bread . . .' ran the gist of his argument. The authorities' response: 'Push off, John.'

Once inside the grassy arena, we selected a few square feet of turf and settled down with our other gallon of cider. Some 150 yards away was a gigantic stage; on the right, portly, bearded roadies bumbled about with bits of wire while on the left Joe Jammer made a horrible racket with lots of guitars. The group stopped, the crowd booed, the Maynard Ferguson Big Band came on to play some sort of jazz music, the crowd booed.

'Hey, people, like there's gonna be a few announcements while, er, the crew shift some gear around,' said the MC to the assembled multitude. 'Like firstly if anyone gets bummed out on a bad trip the Release tent is to the right – that's *your* left, right, heh heh – of the stage. Right. Er, actually, you know, keep it cool with the dope 'cause we have got fuzz out there.' The crowd hissed and booed. 'No, listen, cool it – they're just doing a gig, right. Don't hassle them and they won't hassle you, okay.'

When the MC finally approached the end of this seemingly interminable 'rap', he announced that before the scheduled appearance of Fairport Convention, 'a very special friend would like to come on and sing some songs for free'. To loud groans around the field, Donovan took to the stage.

Two hours into Donovan's enervating set, I realised that I was uncomfortable; the crowd had swelled and my body was now restricted to mere inches of ground. To make matters worse, a stout American

person to my rear kept kicking me – accidentally – in the back. He seemed to be under the influence of something for he was fidgeting about, waving a bent steel coat-hanger in the air. 'What is this *wire*, man?' he kept asking himself loudly. My left leg had gone to sleep so I stood up. 'Hey, sit down, man. I mean, what is this *wire*?' squealed the American. I set off in search of toilet facilities.

Walking across a crowded festival site is a delicate art; the ground is all but obscured by bodies, heads and limbs so one must select one's footing with care. My progress to the latrines was slow and not aided by a lengthy period spent in a queue which, as it turned out, was not for the lavatories at all, but for a hot-dog stand. I got there in the end to find a trench in the ground awash with muck and already stenching furiously. I grappled with mounting nausea.

My trip back to my sacred clump of earth was even slower than the outward journey. I had lost my bearings, such as they were (there are few landmarks among a seething mass of humanity), but once re-united with my party, I swigged cider and

attempted to enjoy the late afternoon's talent parade – Fairport Convention, John Mayall, It's A Beautiful Day, Colosseum – with little success. Then, as Steppenwolf were crunching their way through their anti-US establishment epic, 'Monster', a bleary-eyed hippie stumbled in the dusk, landing on my legs. The pain made me swear. Hippie sat up and blinked. 'Hey, I'm really sorry, man. This festival's got really bad vibes.' He shuffled off in his foul-smelling Afghan coat and his search for who-knows-what.

A psychedelic breakfast

Immense TV screens were beaming the face and guitar of Johnny Winter through the darkness and it was getting cold. Shivering and tired, dirty and bored, I embarked on another tricky trek, to tent and bed. Once inside the welcoming canvas, I

Below: Home on the range – a typically makeshift hippie hovel. Living conditions at large festivals were notoriously squalid and uncomfortable, yet few fans ever complained about the unpleasant sanitary facilities or over-priced food.

found that someone had made off with the cider, the beans, the crisps and the biscuits (but had left the cans of stew – a vegetarian thief obviously). I was too weary to care and so, to the strains of Pink Floyd playing 'Alan's Psychedelic Breakfast' in the distance, I dropped into a deep slumber.

The camp site was a hive of activity as we breakfasted on cold Irish stew – we couldn't get the gas stove to work – the next morning. An evil looking Hell's Angel stalked the grass shouting 'Has anyone got any charge?' in a menacing tone. The

Above: A music-loving gourmet tucks into a nourishing breakfast. Below: Donovan makes an impromptu appearance at Bath; his performance – hardly festival fare – lasted over two hours.

snotty child from the neighbouring tent was playing a game with our guy-ropes while his mother sat cross-legged on an Indian blanket singing Leonard Cohen's 'Suzanne' very badly to the accompaniment of an out-of-tune Spanish guitar. The brat's game reached its conclusion with the

collapse of our tent; 'Bilbo's going through a really destructive stage,' murmured the inept folk-singer.

On our way to the fest field, we passed the Pink Fairies, who were holding an alternative *free* festival on the back of a lorry before a minuscule audience. Meanwhile, on the official stage, Flock were hard at work trying to impress a much larger one with their hideous brand of jazz-rock. Our vantage point this day was even further from the stages than before and just as cramped, but at least I didn't have the feet of the mad coat-hanger fetishist to contend with. Flock made way for Santana made way for Frank Zappa and the Mothers of Invention, but if one had not been paying attention to the MC's announcements one would not have noticed the changes. For a gusty breeze had blown up to whip the sound around like some celestial phasing unit: the music of successive acts had become indistinguishable.

Then appeared the band almost everyone appeared to have been waiting for – Led Zeppelin. The crowd rose to their feet to greet the hard-rock heroes and for the first time the festival turned festive as the throng bounced around and flailed their arms in praise of the heavy-metal din. Which was fine if one *liked* Led Zeppelin – for the minority that did not, however, it was hell. All around me people jerked their limbs, turning their bodies into potentially lethal weapons; there was no escape – I gritted my teeth and tried to ignore the buffets of the idiot dancers.

Low-flying Byrds
Zeppelin screeched through their umpteenth encore – 'Communication Breakdown', I think – and left. So did a sizeable proportion of the crowd; at last I could stretch out on the ground and attain a modicum of comfort. Until, that is, the rains came – just as the band *I* had really come to see were about to begin. Instead of the electric excursions of 'Eight Miles High', 'So You Want To Be A Rock'n'Roll Star' *et al*, the Byrds, through fear of electrocution, performed an acoustic set – better than nothing but a disappointment nonetheless. The water trickled down my neck, seeped through my jeans and into my shoes. I felt damp and miserable. Everyone else felt damp and miserable. Dr John the Night Tripper came on and claimed responsibility – through his voodoo powers – for bringing on the rain. 'Thanks a lot, Doc,' we thought and waded back through the mud to base camp, leaving Jefferson Airplane and the droning MC to their own devices.

Grimy, damp and hungry, more dead than alive, we had braved the elements, endured the discomfort and listened to hours and hours of horrid noisy music we hated for the sake of a couple of enjoyable hours. 'Was it all worth it?' we asked ourselves. 'No,' we replied, 'never again!' But at least the car started: homeward bound, past the tireless Pink Fairies and into the night.   TOM HIBBERT

The Dream Goes Sour

The harsh realities of Altamont and after

*Well I'm going down to Yasgur's Farm/
I'm gonna join in a rock and roll band/
I'm gonna camp out on the land/And set
my soul free . . .*

Idealistic words from Joni Mitchell's 'Woodstock', a song considered by many to express clearly the spirit of the generation that brought new connotations to the 'arts' festival. It reflects, they argue, the atmosphere of relaxed enlightenment that surrounded an aware sub-culture getting to grips with its responsibilities and striving to base an alternative society on mutual trust and understanding.

Although festivals had been in existence since the first stirrings of interest in the performing arts, Woodstock gave strident voice to an idea conceived initially at the 'love-ins', 'be-ins' and 'Trips Festivals' of San Francisco around 1966 and 1967. Here at last was evidence weighty enough to stifle the 'straight' world's snickering accusations of misplaced idealism, a public demonstration of young people's ability to pull together, with *love*, despite it all. Aquarius rising. A new dawn. And so on . . . Here was a generation with a *new* way, embracing radical concerns. The Woodstock Festival was its manifesto.

Yet in many ways Woodstock was a disaster, though most of its bad points got lost in the general backslapping, obscured by sheer relief that no serious calamity occurred during the mud-caked night-

mare. Predictably a number of births were claimed; but the most conspicuous offspring was this peculiarly naive myth of loving togetherness, a cosy notion that would have its awful immaturity exposed only months later. Meredith Hunter's murder at Altamont in December 1969 tore gaping holes in the argument and revealed that alternative societies, too, have their darker side.

Left: Woodstock – three days of peace and love. Below: Altamont – one night of hell. The Angels kill while Their Satanic Majesties play on (bottom).

Bring on the clowns

With the benefit of hindsight, it is obvious that the simple matter of scale was a key factor in the decline of the festival. Although comparatively small affairs, Woodstock's forerunners had had their fair share of problems and it should have been obvious that such organisational difficulties would multiply in direct proportion to the size of the audience. As soon as somebody realised that it was possible to construct a stage in a convenient wide-open space, import all available 'superstars' of the time, jack up the ticket prices and entice hordes of footloose young people from one side of a country to another, there was bound to be trouble. Woodstock, it is true, was eventually declared a 'free' festival but only after circumstances made the organisers' task impossible and forced them to abandon most of their administrative control.

Festivals like Woodstock and the Isle of Wight were a strange and confused mixture of intentions. To the faithful they were wonderful celebrations of noble ideals, a chance to revel in a non-materialistic pantomime while behind the scenes the entire organisational edifice relied on massive financial manipulation to keep it from crumbling. Even then, this commercial wizardry seldom proved successful; Woodstock's organisers went bust faster than their idyllic green pasture turned brown, only to be rescued by the phenomenal box-office receipts earned by the subsequent film of the fracas.

The incongruous wheeling and dealing was distasteful to most of the audience, and was hastily put to the side for better ideals. One of the bitterest pills swallowed by a 1969 Isle of Wight hopeful was the fact that Dylan jetted in, played for his allotted hour and flew out again some 75,000 dollars richer – a vast sum for the times. Out around the campfires with a biting wind howling in the ears, that knowledge did little to warm the bones ... Commercial interest spawned a chill realisation that, already, the 'beautiful' new ideology had succumbed to the lure of capitalism and had been neatly turned upon its creators as the cornerstone of a hugely lucrative industry.

The impact of commercial humiliation, however, was nothing compared to the body-blow that was delivered at Altamont. It seems ironic that human nature should choose a 'free' festival in the very state that acted as midwife at the birth of the 'Woodstock Generation' less than six months earlier at which to bare its bleaker aspect. The Rolling Stones decided to stage a free concert in San Francisco's Golden Gate Park, the intention being to obtain sufficient footage to complete a movie of their 1969 US tour. It proved impracticable to hold the show at that venue, so the concert was re-scheduled for the Sears Point Raceway; with Jefferson Airplane, Crosby, Stills, Nash and Young, Santana and the Flying Burrito Brothers added to the bill, a suitable end sequence for the Maysles

Right: A hippie surrenders to the arms of the law, Windsor 1974. The free festival held in the Great Park was broken up by 600 policemen. Above: More mud than music at Reading, 1975.

Brothers' film looked assured. Problems arose, however, when the proprietors of the raceway realised how many dollars could be generated by a movie of the Stones playing at *their* venue and demanded a slice of the distribution rights. Equally competent at arithmetic, the Stones refused to surrender any interest in the film and, 20 hours before the planned start time, Sears Point pulled out.

Let it bleed

Just as it began to look *too* late, the enterprising proprietor of the Altamont Speedway successfully tempted the Stones to his venue, a barren track surrounded by scrub-encrusted dirthills that more often bore witness to automobile destruction derbies than other, comparatively genteel, pursuits. Due to the short notice, every aspect of the required organisation proved inadequate – most crucially the provision of back-up medical facilities, food supplies and sanitation. To make matters worse, the Stones attracted a far larger crowd than anticipated. And, though so potent a brew hardly needed a catalyst to trigger the inevitable reaction, the Stones' road manager Sam Cutler chose this moment to make the most ill-advised decision of his career. Basing his judgement upon an alleged suggestion by the Grateful Dead and experience of *British* Hell's Angels at an earlier Hyde Park free concert, he hired a bunch of California's 'one per centers' to police the stage. Stoked by copious quantities of dope and alcohol, a day-long atmosphere of unease hung over the crowd, erupting into periodic bouts of brutality around the front-of-stage area which found the available medical aid wanting long before the Stones even began their set.

Much has been made of the Stones' image during this period, Jagger's apparent flirtation with Lucifer being held in some way responsible for the day's bloodshed. Yet at Altamont Jagger seemed powerless and vulnerable, unable to exert his charismatic control over an audience and keep them teetering on the perilous knife-edge between ecstatic adulation and dangerous abandon. There was nothing 'satanic' about rock's fallen angel here and, in truth, the only thing that can be blamed for the whole disaster is an appalling lack of foresight on the part of everyone concerned. Nevertheless, it *was* during the Stones' set that the luckless Hunter drew a pistol to ward off a Hell's Angel who'd already stabbed him at least once, and was promptly dealt with in the most final of fashions. With him died any belief in the 'Woodstock Generation' as a realistic and potent force for change.

Old contemptibles

The blaze of litigation that followed the killing demonstrated once and for all that the unifying force – music – was prone to the same contemptible considerations as the gladiatorial cut-and-thrust of big business in general. As the squalid fit of buck-passing ushered in the new decade it became painfully obvious that nothing had been achieved, nothing was changed. Only the most blinkered defenders of the cause refused to recognise their failure both to confront those considerations and to organise an effective alternative. After Altamont it was only a matter of time before rigor mortis set in and, although the devout continued to attend similar gatherings well into the Seventies, each passing year saw the accent swing farther and farther from the Woodstock blueprint. By the mid Seventies, the balance had tilted irretrievably towards blatant money-spinners, the British examples of which included the large-scale one-day concerts at Knebworth Park, the annual Reading endurance test or Bob Dylan's second outdoor appearance in the UK at Blackbushe Airfield in 1978.

There were exceptions, nonetheless. Those 'hippies' (by now a disparaging term) who had not tired of beating their heads against immovable conventional mores had to be content with low-key gatherings in the shadow of Glastonbury Tor or, at summer solstices, on the wind-blown plain surrounding Stonehenge. Only at such places was there any real remnant of the earlier determination for more tranquil patterns of existence; but instead of being observed anxiously by the society they sought to subvert, they were largely ignored or, at best, regarded with an amused tolerance.   CLIFF ASH

Above right: Reading 1981. A street vendor displays his wares – heavy-metal badges and assorted mementoes. Right: Blackbushe Airfield strewn with litter following Dylan's appearance there on 15th July 1978.

Ready Steady Who!

The marathon career of one of Britain's best-loved bands

BY THEIR VERY NATURE, rock bands have always been transitory phenomena – here today, has-beens tomorrow. And although many of the so-called 'movements' of the Sixties and Seventies have been based on some form of revival or nostalgia, few indeed are the groups that have survived to ride a second wave of success. When Pete Townshend penned 1965's 'My Generation', with its oft-quoted line: 'Hope I die before I get old', he could have had little idea that the Who would survive into the Eighties as a working unit.

Whose generation?
When Pete Townshend, Roger Daltrey, Keith Moon and John Entwistle formed the Who in London in 1964 they started off articulating the feelings and aspirations of a generation – the Mod generation. But Mod was *now*, a hedonistic cult that stressed the immediacy of pleasure, the 'get it while you can' philosophy so succinctly captured by 'My Generation'. Once Mod had run its course, however, the Who were left to sink or swim – and were faced with an ever-widening generation gap between themselves and the teenage frustration that had provided both the basis for their material and the auto-destructive energy of their stage act.

Pete Townshend's answer was *Tommy*, one of the first of rock's many 'concept' albums and one that brought the term 'rock opera' to the lips and pens of many critics. In retrospect, the work seems somewhat hastily thrown together, but at the time it was well-nigh revolutionary. A tour of Europe's opera houses endorsed *Tommy*'s 'legitimate' status as a serious statement in the uncertain musical world of 1969. After the second thoughts of *Live At Leeds*, the Who's eventual return to the concept album format with 1973's *Quadrophenia* confirmed the band's move from youth music into the field of adult rock.

Despite their frequent clashes, the four members of the Who were aware that their spontaneous combustion – when confined to the stage – created pure excitement. 'I don't want to be in a group with anybody else, although if I could choose three friends to go about with, it wouldn't be these three' was singer Roger Daltrey's summary of intra-group relations. The Who was quite simply the best vehicle for the songs of Pete Townshend, but by 1980's *Empty Glass* album, the guitarist had grown in confidence to such an extent that his future as a solo artist seemed more promising than the Who's own career.

The punk/new wave movement of the late Seventies owed much to the Who. Aside from the steals – the Sex Pistols' raucous version of 'Substitute' – and overt homage from groups like the Jam, it was the *attitude* that carried over. Yet the mass outrage and sensational

press coverage of punk echoed the Who's earlier career and must have led them to question their continued existence, especially when drummer Keith Moon died in 1978.

The casting of Sting (of the Police) as the Ace Face in the film version of *Quadrophenia* was perhaps symbolic of the Who's inevitable eclipse by new idols. They have never settled comfortably into the roles of elder statesmen, however. The band's early-Eighties split and subsequent on-off reformations suggest that this situation is likely to continue. Despite personal antipathies, they realise their mix of musical talents remains greater than the sum of its parts.   MICHAEL HEATLEY

Out in the street. In the late Seventies, the Jam (below) based much of their music, act and image on that of the early Who (above). But while the Jam elected to split up in 1982, the Who – despite constant rumour to the contrary – continued.
The Who's on-off Eighties career of splits and reformations hardly gilded the legend.

WHO DIARY

1944
1 March   Roger Harry Daltrey born, Hammersmith, London.
9 October   John Alec Entwistle born, Chiswick, London.

1945
19 May   Peter Dennis Blandford Townshend born, Chiswick, London.

1947
23 August   Keith John Moon born, Wembley, Middlesex.

1948
16 September   Kenneth Jones born, Stepney, London.

1962
Roger Daltrey forms the Detours, a skiffle group, enlisting Entwistle in the summer. Rhythm guitarist Pete Townshend is later added at Entwistle's suggestion.

1964
Keith Moon joins the Detours after an impromptu audition at the Oldfield Hotel, Greenford.
3 July   'I'm The Face'/'Zoot Suit', credited to the High Numbers, released on the Fontana label. Both sides are written and produced by manager Pete Meaden.
September   Kit Lambert and Chris Stamp buy out Meaden's contract after seeing the High Numbers at Watford Trade Hall.
24 November   Re-named the Who, the band start a 16-week residency at London's Marquee Club. 200 people attend first night, but sell-out attendances soon follow.

1965
15 January   John Entwistle resigns from the Inland Revenue on the release of 'I Can't Explain'. Produced by Shel Talmy, the record reaches Number 8 in UK. It appears on Brunswick.
21 May   Group promote 'Anyway, Anyhow, Anywhere' on ITV's 'Ready, Steady, Go!'; the programme later selects it as its theme tune.
4 September   The band's van is stolen from outside Battersea Dogs Home. It is recovered later – minus £5,000 worth of equipment.
27 November   'My Generation' reaches Number 2 in UK – the nearest the Who ever get to the top slot.
December   The Brunswick label releases the Who's first LP, *My Generation*.

1966
March   Keith Moon marries model Kim Kerrigan in secret ceremony.
28 August   First Kit Lambert-produced single released on the Reaction label. Entitled 'I'm A Boy', it reaches Number 2.
3 December   The band's second album, *A Quick One*, contains songs written by all four members.

1967
22 March   The Who fly to US – where the single 'Happy Jack' is about to chart – to appear in disc jockey Murray the K's show at Brooklyn's Fox Theatre.
22 April   'Pictures Of Lily' is released on Lambert and Stamp's new Track label.
18 June   The Who's auto-destructive stage act astounds the crowds at the Monterey Pop Festival.
23 June   John Entwistle marries Alison Wise: they honeymoon on the *Queen Elizabeth*.
30 June   The Who cover the Rolling Stones' 'The Last Time'/'Under My Thumb' as a gesture of solidarity with the imprisoned Mick Jagger and Keith Richards. With Entwistle still on honeymoon, Townshend plays bass.
July/August   Seven-week tour of the US with Herman's Hermits and the Blues Magoos.
23 August   Holiday Inn at Flint, Michigan, is venue for Keith Moon's 21st birthday party. Bill for damage caused amounts to 24,000 dollars.

14 October   'I Can See For Miles' released; it features in the Top Ten on both sides of the Atlantic.
November   The Who pay tribute to fast-fading pirate radio with *The Who Sell Out*.

1968
20 May   Pete Townshend marries Karen Astley at Didcot, Berkshire.
June   'Dogs'/'Call Me Lightning' single proves a rare flop, failing to make the UK Top Thirty altogether.
20 November   Final date of UK tour at Liverpool's Empire Theatre sees Keith Moon and drummer Kenney Jones of support group the Small Faces play together on 'Magic Bus' encore.
12 December   The Who take part in the Rolling Stones' abortive 'Rock'n'Roll Circus' TV spectacular.

1969
2 May   *Tommy* is previewed live for the UK press at Ronnie Scott's jazz club in Soho, London.
16 May   Townshend is arrested in New York after kicking plain-clothes police officer Daniel Mulhearn on stage at the Fillmore East; Mulhearn had got up to warn the audience of a fire in an adjoining building and Townshend mistook him for a fan. Fined 75 dollars.
17 August   Who climax Woodstock with a performance in the early hours of Sunday morning.
14 December   Tour of European opera houses commences at the London Coliseum.

1970
4 January   Keith Moon's chauffeur Neil Boland killed in bizarre accident when drummer opened disco at Hatfield, Hertfordshire.
May   *Live At Leeds* issued in plain cover designed to imitate an unauthorised bootleg recording.
November   Track Records compile an album of Entwistle compositions from the Who's previous releases, entitled *The Ox*.

1971

25 June   Release of 'Won't Get Fooled Again', a post-Woodstock statement of disillusionment. Recorded at Stargroves (Mick Jagger's residence), it makes the UK Number 9 position.

July   The Glyn Johns-produced *Who's Next* becomes first Who LP since *My Generation* not to have been produced by Kit Lambert.

18 September   35,000 crowd gathers at Surrey's Oval cricket ground for 'Goodbye Summer', a concert for Bangladesh featuring the Who, Atomic Rooster, Mott the Hoople and Lindisfarne.

11 December   'Let's See Action' reaches the UK Number 16 position.

1972

February/March   Townshend makes pilgrimage to tomb of Meher Baba in India.

October   *Who Came First*, Townshend's first solo album, emerges. It reflects many aspects of his recently found faith. Lou Reizner production of *Tommy* released. Record features the London

Symphony Orchestra and Chamber Chorus.

June   'Join Together' released. Features a live B-side, 'Baby Don't You Do It', written by Motown's Holland-Dozier-Holland team and previously recorded by Marvin Gaye.

November   Keith Moon joins cast of *That'll Be The Day* for filming at Isle of Wight.
'Relay' becomes the third Who single in succession not lifted from an album. B-side 'Waspman' is a Keith Moon composition.

1973

January   Eric Clapton's return to public performance at the Rainbow Theatre is masterminded by Pete Townshend, who plays rhythm guitar in Clapton's all-star backup band.

November   *Quadrophenia*, a two album set with integral booklet, released.

20 November   Keith Moon collapses at the drums during opening gig of a US tour in San Francisco. 19-year-old Scott Halpin deputises for last three numbers.

2 December   Who and entourage spend night in jail after Montreal hotel suite is wrecked.

1974

12 April   Pete Townshend plays his first solo concert, for charity, at London's Roundhouse.

22 April   Filming of *Tommy* begins.

June   80,000 seats sold within hours for four concerts at New York's Madison Square Gardens.

October   *Odds And Sods*, a collection of mostly unreleased material, issued. Cut-out cover has text in Braille as well as normal script.

1975

January   John Entwistle starts tour with his occasional band Ox. It ends in March amid recriminations and debt.

April   Kim Moon divorces Keith.

May   *Two Sides Of The Moon*, the drummer's first solo album, struggles to the record racks but hits the bargain bins shortly after.

October   *The Who By Numbers* is first Who album to appear on the Polydor label.

20 November   Entwistle and lighting engineer John Wolff arrested in Houston,

Texas, after opening tour party gets out of hand. The 18 US concerts played grossed over three million dollars.

1976

February   'Squeeze Box' gives the Who a now-rare UK Top Ten entry. It stays in the charts for 9 weeks.

April   Peter Rudge makes way for Bill Curbishley as band manager.

31 May   The Who's concert at Charlton football ground earns them an entry in the *Guinness Book of Records* as the 'world's loudest pop group', with a 120-decibel reading at 50 metres.

1977

September   *Rough Mix*, an album of songs from Pete Townshend and ex-Face Ronnie Lane, makes a low-key but welcome appearance.

December   Concert at Kilburn State Theatre for filming marks Keith Moon's last live appearance.

1978

August   *Who Are You* released.

12 August   Former manager Peter Meaden found dead.

8 September   Keith Moon dies in Harry Nilsson's Mayfair flat. An open verdict was recorded.

1979

2 May   Return to live performance at London's Rainbow Theatre with John 'Rabbit' Bundrick (ex-Free) on keyboards and former Faces drummer Kenney Jones.

June   *The Kids Are Alright*, a mostly live double LP, released to tie in with documentary film of same name.

3 December   11 die at Cincinnati's Riverfront Coliseum when crowd stampede buries fans.

28 December   The Who play at Concerts for Kampuchea at Hammersmith Odeon, and contribute four tracks to the resulting album. Townshend also plays in Paul McCartney's Rockestra the following night – he is the only member to refuse to wear the group's 'glitter-suit' uniform.

1980

14 April   *Empty Glass*, Townshend's first solo album since *Who Came First*, released on the Atco label to rave reviews.

May   Premiere of *McVicar* at Cannes Film Festival. Acclaimed as Roger Daltrey's best movie performance to date.

1981

February   The Who make rare appearance on BBC-TV's 'Top Of The Pops' to promote new single 'You Better You Bet' in the middle of their longest-ever British tour.

March   *Face Dances* appears in sleeve collage of 16 portraits of Townshend, Daltrey, Entwistle and Jones by 16 different artists.

7 April   Death of Kit Lambert, the Who's manager in the Sixties.

1982

June   Townshend releases *All The Best Cowboys Have Chinese Eyes*, his third official solo album.

20 August   Daltrey announces that the Who's current US tour will be their last. 'Being on the road is hard work,' he commented.

September   Cover of Who's *It's Hard* shows child playing video machine in echo of *Tommy*.

1984

Belated release of live *Who's Last*—two years after the final tour.

1985

13 July   Live Aid prompts a temporary Who reformation for a 17-minute set. "We always said we'd never play together again," said Townshend, "and we always meant it. But it would have been kind of difficult not to get together again for this day."

1988

February   Who reunion at the British Phonographic Industry award ceremony in London is followed by talk of an album.

MICHAEL HEATLEY

How four individual talents hit the top

THE VOLATILE ELEMENTS that constitute the Who have fuelled more break-up rumours than any of Elizabeth Taylor's marriages, and yet the group has survived intact, save for one untimely death. What's more, they've done so – give or take a synthesiser or two – with little alteration to their essential style.

The Who's beginning was as unexceptional as that of any of the countless groups that emerged all over Britain in the early Sixties. Pete Townshend (born 19 May 1945) and John Entwistle (born 9 October 1944) went to the same West London grammar school and first played together – on banjo and trumpet respectively – in a traditional jazz band, switching to amplified acoustic guitar and electric bass and Shadows instrumentals, before they joined an expelled former schoolmate, Roger Daltrey (born 1 March 1944), in the Detours. Daltrey was the lead guitarist until the Beatles made vocal numbers an acceptable part of groups' repertoires and he switched to singing. The drummer, Doug Sandom, was some years older and looked it, a disadvantage that, along with his lack of expertise on the kit, got him

kicked out in 1964. At a gig in Greenford with a temporary replacement they were approached by Keith Moon (born 23 August 1947), a pushy 17-year-old, drunk in a ginger suit and matching haircut, who auditioned on the spot and damaged the drumkit; Moon got the job.

High numbers

By then the Beatles songbook had been dropped for R&B, and the group had broken out of their suburban circuit of pubs and halls to play in the West End at the Scene Club. The Detours had become the Who, and then the High Numbers, this last name chosen by their then-manager Peter Meaden, an arch-Mod who had hustled them the Wednesday residency at the Scene, centre of the Mods' musical universe.

The Mod cult was mushrooming, and Meaden was keen to create a group with whom all Mods could identify; he kitted them out in Carnaby Street gear and took them to a hairdresser who knew a French crew from a college boy. Meaden moulded the image better than the music, however. He brashly rewrote Slim Harpo's 'Got Love If You Want It' as 'I'm The Face' and produced the record with the equally fashion-fixated 'Zoot Suit' on the flip for Fontana, but this first single failed to convey the excitement of the group on stage and it flopped when it was released in July 1964.

Although the Who's business association with Peter Meaden was, like the name he gave them, short-lived, his influence was considerable, for the Mod lifestyle to which he introduced the group was Pete Townshend's initial inspiration as a songwriter. The band returned to their home patch on the western fringes of London, where their reputation for musical mayhem brought crowds to every performance. It was the queue outside the Railway Hotel in Wealdstone that prompted Kit Lambert to go inside and listen to the group who were playing there, but it was what he saw and heard on the small stage that took him to see them again the following night at Watford with his partner Chris Stamp.

Lambert and Stamp were assistant film directors on the lookout for a suitable small-time group around which to base a documentary. Instead, they ended up days later as the Who's managers, and the money they had pooled to finance their film was used to promote their protégés.

Left: The High Numbers at the Scene Club, 1964, shortly before changing their name back to the Who. Below: Moon hits out.

The music the group played was basically the same brand of R&B as before, but the aggression on stage had increased. Pete Townshend's attitude to an instrument most guitarists treated with respect or even awe was loutish, as if trying to master it by brute force where he failed by guile; and Keith Moon's excesses egged him on. Also, Townshend had started writing songs.

Maximum R&B

The group's first single as the Who, 'I Can't Explain', was released in January 1965. A Townshend composition, the song was produced by Shel Talmy and the sound of the record was clearly borrowed from the Kinks' 'You Really Got Me', an earlier Talmy production. A second assault on the West End was already under way on Tuesday nights at the Marquee in Wardour Street, Lambert and Stamp having ensured a return booking at the club by distributing half-price and free tickets among the Who's hardcore Shepherd's Bush followers for the first appearance at the new venue.

This residency was publicised by a memorable white-on-black poster promising 'Maximum R&B' with Townshend in characteristic birdman pose flailing his Rickenbacker and an arrow rising from the 'o' of Who. It was a powerful image to mirror the power of the music.

The Marquee was an important club in the mid Sixties and, as such, had become a source of up-and-coming acts for independent television's trendy 'Ready, Steady, Go!' pop show, which was networked each Friday evening. The Who duly appeared on the show to promote 'I Can't Explain' in front of a studio audience that had been infiltrated by the group's fans, and subsequent sales took the record into the Top Thirty for a single week in February. It wasn't until they got a spot on BBC-TV's 'Top Of The Pops' that the single really took off, however. It entered the Top Twenty in the last week of March and eventually reached Number 8.

The moment was precisely right for the Who's image. The Mod cult had begun as a secret society, a narcissistic and impenetrable élite with a shared taste in sharp clothes, black music and amphetamines, but by 1965, thanks to 'Ready, Steady, Go!' and an expanding chain of Carnaby Street-based clothing boutiques, it was just one more form of teenage consumerism. The original Mods had moved on to other kinds of self-expression, but there were kids who called themselves Mods in towns all over the country, all of them wearing the proscribed style of clothes and all of them looking for a band to identify with. Their predecessors had invented their own fashions and

found their own music in American record catalogues; they had created their own Mod lifestyle. The new would-be Mod masses had the lot marketed to them. From Peter Meaden, via Lambert and Stamp, they got the Who.

The allegiance of the Who's management to the Mod movement was minimal. For them it was simply a means of acquiring a ready-made audience for their group's music. By the time the second single, 'Anyway, Anyhow, Anywhere', came out in May, they had adopted a new sales strategy: Pop Art. Pop Art was Pete Townshend in a jacket tailored from a Union Jack, Moon with a target on his T-shirt, Daltrey with strips of sticky tape on his jumper, Entwistle in militaria. Pop Art was a promotional gimmick and it worked superbly. The newspapers fell for it in a big way, devoting double-page spreads to the supposed phenomenon. 'Anyway, Anyhow, Anywhere', of course, became the Who's second Top Ten hit.

A mental block

But Mod had meant more to Townshend. He had admired Meaden and the other 'faces', had been influenced by Guy Stevens' collection of American records and he got blocked up to the eyeballs, as the vernacular had it, on stimulants: blues, dexies, black bombers and the rest. An earnest television interviewer inquired, at the time, if the group's alleged affection for pills meant they were blocked when they went on stage sometimes. 'No,' Townshend replied, deadpan, 'it means we're blocked *all* the time.'

As Mod gathered momentum, a face other than vanity was shown – a face that wore a violent expression. The Mods' boyish haircuts and clothes-consciousness hid the truth that they were some of the hardest people about. The Mods-versus-Rockers seaside riots, of which the press made so much, were mostly one-sided: the leather-jacketed greasers were usually the ones sprinting across the sand away from a beating.

When skinheads later earned an appropriate reputation for violence, their bristling crops and boots made it easy to accept. But Mods kicked heads in expensive Italian shoes. Most observers had got it wrong, assuming the rockers were the aggressors; Townshend knew otherwise. His early songs conveyed the aimless aggression of the Mods in their lyrics and their music. 'Anyway, Anyhow, Anywhere' (co-written with Daltrey) contained an extraordinary instrumental expression of violence in Townshend's guitar solo, its electric staccato created by switching between the two pickups on his guitar. On stage he scraped the strings across the mikestand or caused howls of feedback by shoving the instrument at the speaker cabinet. And he smashed guitars as part of his performance.

'My Generation', released at the end of October, was the culmination of Townshend's Mod-oriented songs. There was

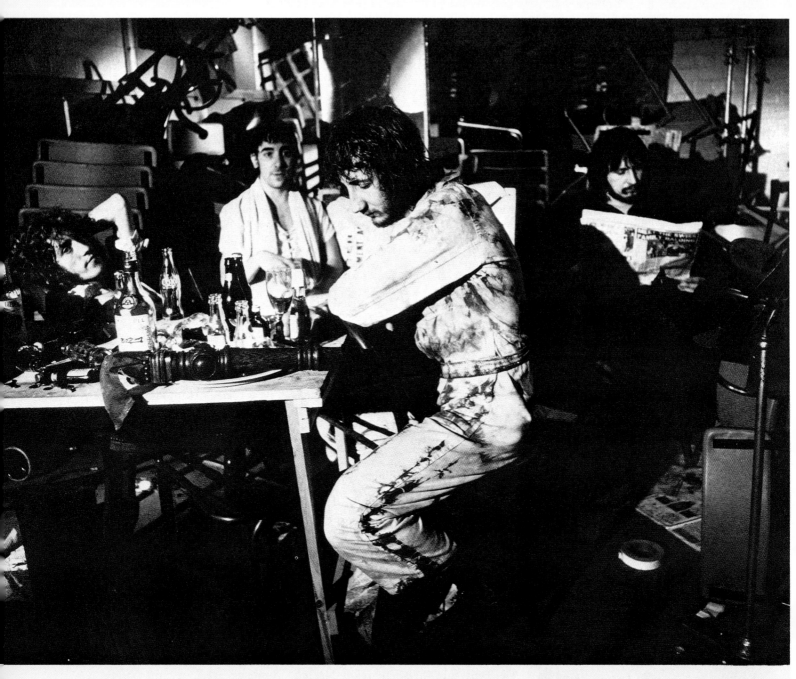

enough feedback on the track to convince the group's American record company that the recording was faulty, but this time it was the words that encapsulated the anger and alienation: 'People try to put us down/ Just because we get around/Things they do look awful cold/Hope I die before I get old (talking 'bout my generation).' Plenty of kids identified with Townshend's anthem, which only just missed Number 1 in December.

Although the success of three major hit singles in nine months had established the Who as a significant new force in British pop, the group's future at the end of 1965 was as shaky as it ever would be. Townshend might boast to journalists, 'We don't get on together – and we prefer it that way,' but relationships within the 'group with built-in hate' rocked dangerously. Roger Daltrey was rumoured to be on his way out; Townshend and Kit Lambert discussed the possibility of continuing as a three-piece or

combining with another trio, Paddy, Klaus and Gibson; and Entwistle later admitted that he and Moon had considered forming a group, tentatively named Led Zeppelin.

Certainly there were reasons for rifts other than personality clashes and Daltrey's readiness to argue with his knuckles. After all, the group that had started out as his was now dominated by Townshend: indeed, a creative process had been established that Townshend and the Who would stick to. He had installed enough studio equipment in his flat to make demos of his songs (published by his own company, Fabulous Music Ltd) with guitar, bass, drums and vocals, which were distributed to the other members of the group before each recording session. Usually the arrangements hardly altered.

The unsettled atmosphere that enveloped the group was made more menacing by a dispute with their producer and their record company. An album, *My*

Generation, produced by Shel Talmy, was issued by Decca in December 1965 and went to Number 5, but three months later the Who's next single, 'Substitute', credited Kit Lambert as producer – though Townshend was the prime creative force – and appeared on Polydor's new Reaction label, set up by the group's agent, Robert Stigwood.

'Substitute' was a different style of song from the Pete Townshend compositions used as A-sides on the Who's previous singles. The character at the centre of those songs had been him (or someone like him), but not so the first person in 'Substitute'. The lyric was impersonal and clever; whereas Roger Daltrey had sung Townshend's 'Hope I die before I get old' line as if he meant it, the neat juxtapositions of 'Substitute' demanded a less obsessive delivery. The next three singles introduced subjects and themes that were not only new to the group, but were far from the conventional pop formula—confused sexuality ('I'm A Boy'), a seaside donkey ('Happy Jack') and sex fantasy ('Pictures of Lily')—yet all three were Top Five hits in the UK.

Encouraged by Kit Lambert, however, Pete Townshend's ambitions were expanding. He had mastered the essential pop form (the single) and was turning his attention to albums. The Who's first album, *My Generation*, pinpointed the group's transition from R&B to a style of their own built on Townshend's growing songwriting talent. All that remained of the R&B repertoire, which Roger Daltrey was so reluctant to abandon, were two James Brown numbers and Muddy Waters' 'I'm A Man'. The Townshend tracks were taking over.

Nine-minute opera

The second album, *A Quick One*, released in December 1966, contained only one non-original, their frenetic cover of Martha and the Vandellas' 'Heat Wave', but in order to comply with the terms of a new publishing deal all four members of the group provided material. Although John Entwistle's quirky 'Boris The Spider' was good enough to have been included anyway, the Townshend tracks were predictably better than the rest. Most impressive was a nine-minute song cycle, 'A Quick One While He's Away'.

The theme of infidelity was as simple as the score, but it suggested there was more to come, and within a matter of months Townshend was talking of his intention to devote an entire double album to a pop opera. Each time the subject came up in successive interviews the story or the title tended to change, but the project remained prominent among Townshend's plans and eventually appeared in 1969 as *Tommy*.

Uppermost among the reasons for this long period of incubation was what made the Who as popular as they were: their live work. Unlike the Beatles, who stopped touring in August 1966, and the Rolling

Stones, who cut back their performances later that year, the Who knew they were at their best on stage. Even when Townshend wasn't smashing his guitar or Moon kicking over his kit, their act could be awe-inspiring.

In 1967 they took it to America, where they upset Herman's Hermits' fans as support act on a seven-week slog, and pulled out all the stops at the Monterey Pop Festival. Before the end of the year they had enough fans in the States to make 'I Can See For Miles' their first US Top Ten hit. That single was the closest the Who had come to psychedelia, but it was in fact an old recording kept 'in the can' in case they ran out of singles, as indeed they did. It also reappeared on *The Who Sell Out* (1967), a gimmicky album, full of ideas but poorly executed.

Left: The Who booze it up at a photo session. Above: Maximum R&B on TV. Below left: The young Who pose in Mod gear. Below right: After Keith Moon's death in 1978, Kenney Jones (second from left) joined the band as his replacement.

The time spent on *Tommy* and on tour affected the group's status as a successful singles band, and when 'Pinball Wizard' was issued in March 1969, as an appetiser for the ambitious rock opera, they hadn't had a record in the Top Twenty on either side of the Atlantic since 'I Can See For Miles' in December 1967. Ironically, with the exception of 'Pinball Wizard' (and in America 'See Me, Feel Me' as well), *Tommy* did little to change that situation, because its unprecedented success elevated them to the album market. The story of the 'deaf, dumb and blind kid' who 'sure plays a mean pinball' made them rich and it made them respectable. They performed it in opera houses, where it was reviewed by intellectuals. They performed it at Woodstock but their performance was a miserable one and the Who soon longed to drop *Tommy* from their act.

Within a year of the album's release, they got their feet back on more familiar ground with the issue of a live set recorded not at the New York Met or any of the other distinguished auditoriums they had lately appeared in, but Leeds University.

Who's in the Lifehouse?

Live At Leeds was packaged in a plain, functional sleeve, stapled together and packed with memorabilia from earlier days: a date sheet, a contract cancellation, a record company rejection letter, a threat over unpaid HP. The live music itself was a reminder that however clever the Who had become, they hadn't forgotten the basics: they could still play loud rock'n'roll when they wanted or were given the chance.

Tommy remained a tough act to follow, however, and Pete Townshend spent much mental energy working on an even more ambitious project, tentatively titled *Lifehouse*. However, his ideas for this new project seemed vague and confused, to say the least – '*Lifehouse* is like a theatre. It is about a group and about music and about experiments and about concerts and about a day when a concert emerges that is so incredible that the whole audience disappears,' he stated. In the end, *Lifehouse* was aborted as impractical though some of the written material was salvaged for *Who's Next* (1971). Townshend himself thought the new LP was 'ordinary' but it did contain some moments of inspired hard rock, particularly in the powerful 'Won't Get Fooled Again' which was edited for single release and made Number 9 in the UK and Number 15 in the States.

Like *Lifehouse*, the group's next elaborate project, *Quadrophenia* – planned partly to take over from *Tommy* as the central section of their live set – could not readily be transposed to the stage. Moreover, the way the four-way split in the personality of the central character in this homage to the Mod lifestyle was represented by the four members of the group – Daltrey the tough, Townshend the hypocrite, Entwistle the romantic and Moon the loon – pertinently reflected the state of the Who in this post-*Tommy* era. Townshend and Daltrey were feuding regularly (and even came to blows during the recording of *Quadrophenia*), while the group members were embarking on an increasing number of solo projects.

Each recorded on his own, John Entwistle most prolifically, Roger Daltrey most successfully – 'Giving It All Away', a single culled from his 1973 *Daltrey* album, reached Number 5 in the UK. Daltrey, for so long no more than Pete Townshend's mouthpiece, made the most of the Seventies, using his starring role in Ken Russell's screen version of *Tommy* (1975) as a springboard to a screen career. The various individual interests of the Who's members affected the group itself, and *The Who By Numbers* (1975) was an oddly introspective album, while *Who Are You* (1978) lacked inspiration.

A few weeks after the release of *Who Are You* the group was almost stopped in its tracks by the death of Keith Moon on 8 September 1978. The previous evening Moon had been at a party thrown by Paul McCartney in honour of Buddy Holly's birthday. He had appeared to be in high spirits and had announced his engagement to girlfriend Annette Walter-Lax. Following an early breakfast the next morning, Keith swallowed a number of pills and fell into a sleep from which he never awoke. According to the autopsy, an overdose of the sedative drug Heminevrin – prescribed for Moon's alcoholism – was responsible for the death. Whatever the cause, the years of reckless living had finally taken their toll.

Who's on stage? Opposite, clockwise from top left: Keith Moon; Kenney Jones; Pete Townshend; John Entwistle. Below: With microphone held aloft, Roger Daltrey strikes a typical stage pose.

Four days after Moon's death, Pete Townshend issued an official statement regarding future group plans. 'We have lost our great comedian, the supreme melodramatist, the man who apart from being the most unpredictable and spontaneous drummer in rock, would have set himself alight if he thought it would make the audience laugh or jump out of its seats . . . The Who? We are more determined than ever to carry on and we want the spirit of the group to which Keith contributed so much to go on, although no human being can ever take his place.' In the event, Kenney Jones, ex-drummer of the Small Faces and the Faces, was recruited as a permanent replacement, with keyboardist John 'Rabbit' Bundrick added for live performances.

Pete Townshend had apparently retained the greatest interest in the Who in the Seventies. His own solo efforts had seemed no more than throwaways, his best songs always saved for the group, but there was nothing half-hearted about *Empty Glass*, released in April 1980 and a bestseller in the States that year. The disappointing *Face Dances* (1982) was the group's last studio album, the final vinyl *Who's Last* being a memento of their 1982 US tour. But to the surprise of all, they reformed first to play at Live Aid in 1985 and then in February 1988 to receive a British Phonographic Industry award celebrating 25 years of the Who. But harmony appeared short-lived, and no new product emerged that year.   JOHN PIDGEON

During the Seventies, the Who began to incorporate a dazzling laser display into their spectacular stage show.

THE WHO
Discography to 1982

Singles
As the High Numbers
I'm The Face/Zoot Suit (Fontana TF 480, 1964)

As the Who
I Can't Explain/Bald Headed Woman (Brunswick 05926, 1965); Anyway, Anyhow, Anywhere/Daddy Rolling Stone (Brunswick 05935, 1965); My Generation/Shout And Shimmy (Brunswick 05944, 1965); Substitute/Circles (Reaction 591001, 1966); Substitute/Instant Party (Reaction 591001, 1966); A Legal Matter/Instant Party (Brunswick 05956, 1966); Substitute/Waltz For A Pig (Reaction 591001, 1966); The Kids Are Alright/The Ox (Brunswick 05965, 1966); I'm A Boy/In The City (Reaction 591004, 1966); La La La La Lies/The Good's Gone (Brunswick 05968, 1966); Happy Jack/I've Been Away (Reaction 591010, 1966); Pictures Of Lily/Doctor Doctor (Track 604 002, 1967); The Last Time/Under My Thumb (Track 604 006, 1967); I Can See For Miles/Someone's Coming (Track 604 011, 1967); Dogs/Call Me Lightning (Track 604 023, 1968); Magic Bus/Dr Jekyll And Mr Hyde (Track 604 024, 1968); Pinball Wizard/Dogs Part II (Track 604 027, 1969); The Seeker/Here For More (Track 604 036, 1969); Summertime Blues/Heaven And Hell (Track 2094 002, 1970); See Me, Feel Me/Overture From Tommy (Track 2094 004, 1970); Won't Get Fooled Again/Don't Know Myself (Track 2094 009, 1971); Let's See Action/When I Was A Boy (Track 2094 012, 1971); Join Together/Baby, Don't You Do It (Track 2094 102, 1972); Relay/Waspman (Track 2094 106, 1972); 5.15/Water (Track 2094 115, 1973); Squeeze Box/Success Story (Polydor 2121 275, 1976); Who Are You/Had Enough (Polydor WHO 1, 1978); Long Live Rock/I'm The Face/My Wife (Polydor WHO 2, 1979); 5.15/I'm One (Polydor WHO 3, 1979); You Better You Bet/The Quiet One (Polydor WHO 4, 1981); Don't Let Go The Coat/You (Polydor WHO 5, 1981); Athena/A Man Is A Man (Polydor WHO 6, 1982).

EPs
Ready Steady Who! (Reaction 592001, 1966); *Tommy* (Track 2252 001, 1970).

Albums
My Generation (Brunswick LAT 8616, 1965); *A Quick One* (Reaction 593 002, 1966); *The Who Sell Out* (Track 613 002, 1967); *Direct Hits* (Track 613 006, 1968); *Tommy* (Track 613 013/4, 1969); *Live At Leeds* (Track 2406 001, 1970); *Who's Next* (Track 2408 102, 1971); *Meaty, Beaty, Big And Bouncy* (Track 2406 006, 1971); *Quadrophenia* (Track 2657 013, 1973); *Odds And Sods* (Track 2406 116, 1974); *The Who By Numbers* (Polydor 2490 129, 1975); *The Story Of The Who* (Polydor 2683 069, 1976); *Who Are You* (Polydor WHOD 5004, 1978); *The Kids Are Alright* (Polydor 2675 179, 1979); *Quadrophenia* (soundtrack) (Polydor 2625 037, 1979); *Face Dances* (Polydor WHOD 5037, 1981); *Phases* (Nine-album boxed set) (Polydor 2675 216, 1981); *It's Hard* (Polydor WHOD 5066, 1982).

From Mod beginnings right up to the Eighties, (top and above), the Who's live act has remained a phenomenal experience.

Mods and Rock Operas

From television to Tommy and the big screen

IF EVER THERE has been a group made for film, it is the Who; their film connections go back much earlier than *Quadrophenia, The Kids Are Alright*, or even *Tommy* – all of which appeared in the Seventies – yet their contributions to rock cinema are all too often overlooked.

Film, even the starkest documentary, is about creating an image. Early rock'n'roll, perhaps echoing the halcyon days of Hollywood, emphasised individual images: Elvis, Jerry Lee Lewis, Little Richard. And while not the first, the Who were one of the most efficient bands at creating a group image. One of their earliest managers, Pete Meaden, began the process by moulding them, as the High Numbers, into a Mod band. Individual names were not as important as the right style, clothes, hair, music—the right image.

Electric flash

That they were masters very early on in creating a powerful image is demonstrated by their initial involvement with Kit Lambert and Chris Stamp, the Who's main managers through the Sixties. In mid 1964, Lambert and Stamp were young film directors who wanted to make a film that captured rock's visual element. Lambert came across the High Numbers while looking for a group for the film and, though he knew little or nothing about rock, was impressed with their impact on their audience. Instead of making the film, Lambert and Stamp took over the band's management and quickly began to expand their image. Whether it was stacking amps on top of each other, putting tiny speakers in huge, flashy cabinets, smashing a guitar whenever a member of the press happened to be around, or mouthing outrageous statements about 'auto-destruction' and 'Pop Art', the early Who used every theatrical trick available to promote themselves.

Considering the film background of Lambert and Stamp, it is not surpris-

ing to find that many Who singles were backed with a promotional film. These clips seldom got wide distribution but are clearly the forerunners of the video explosion of the Eighties; in the films for 'Happy Jack' and 'Cobwebs And Strange', for example, the group acted out a storyline to the music instead of simply miming to the songs. Some 13 years later, videos for singles were to become commonplace.

Out of focus

Likewise, the Who's appearances on various TV shows were masterpieces, the lessons of which have been largely ignored by cinema rock. After years of attempting to portray the visual experience of a live act, the rock camera still persists in focusing primarily on whoever is singing, while the Who's filmed performances on 'Ready, Steady, Go!' and 'Shindig', clearly show how narrow such an approach is. Moon is pulling faces and twirling drumsticks, Townshend is leaping around and scowling as if each note is an electric shock, and even Entwistle's 'oh-so-bored' look demands attention. Daltrey *has* to smash his mike into the floor to hold the cameraman's attention.

Such tensions seemed a natural choice for a major film effort and there are several documented efforts to do just that. While filming his version of Swinging London, Michelangelo Antonioni approached the

The Who on Brighton beach, the mid-Sixties setting for Mod/Rocker skirmishes that would be re-enacted on film in Quadrophenia.

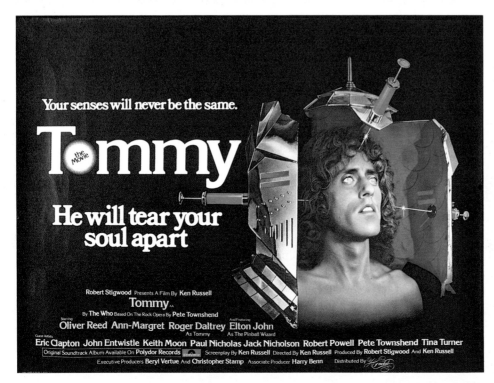

Conceptual motion

Promo clips for singles continued to be made, but the Who's next project was to exhibit greater visual potential. When it was released in May 1969, it soon became apparent that *Tommy* was something special. And as early as July 1969, *Melody Maker* reported that *Tommy* was going to be made into a film. Track Records (Lambert and Stamp's company) was quoted as saying the backing was provided by Universal Studios (owners of the Who's American record company). Track was to provide a script and the Who's exact role was left to be worked out later. Lambert did produce a screenplay, but it didn't get a completely positive response at Universal, where it became entangled in a two-year bureaucratic snarl before finally being rejected.

After years of wrangling, Tommy *(left) was finally released in 1975. Although the film received mixed reviews, Daltrey's performance was much praised, as was his acting in* McVicar *(below). Bottom: Scooter boys rev up in a scene from* Quadrophenia.

Who to perform in one scene. Negotiations broke down, however, and, on its release in 1966, the movie *Blow Up* showed Jeff Beck leading the Yardbirds through a Pete Townshend impersonation of smashing up a guitar. Early 1967 saw the public announcement of a Who TV show, possibly involving cartoon animation. But by May 1967, all plans were off as the Who began their first major assault on America – besides, the Monkees and their TV series had shown that such an idea was no longer acceptable in serious rock circles.

The Who did appear on film, however, in *Monterey Pop* (1968). Although only the climactic 'My Generation' was included, the power and fury of the early Who was clearly shown and remains the highpoint of the film. Yet even this performance from June 1967 is another manifestation of the Who's extraordinary ability to create an image. For, by this time, the Who had dropped 'auto-destruction' and 'Pop Art' from UK performances. As one weekly music paper reported, the Who must have felt they were going back through time by resurrecting old tricks for new American audiences.

The repercussions of this incident were far-reaching. The Who became bored with *Tommy* and wanted to move on to something new before the deaf, dumb and blind kid consumed the group. Pete Townshend and Kit Lambert grew disenchanted with each other: Townshend feeling that Lambert was the reason the film project had come to a halt, Lambert failing to understand Townshend's need to create something new instead of milking *Tommy* for as long as possible. Townshend was also now in the somewhat unenviable position of being hailed as a rock genius and generation spokesman.

In this atmosphere there was no-one to tell Townshend when his ideas outran technical possibilities. He began developing a science-fiction theme known as *Lifehouse* in which, Townshend believed, the Who and their audience would be ensconced together for a period of time and eventually, by feeding biological, astrological and other pertinent information into a computer, would discover the perfect note to bring everyone into one cosmic union. If the idea sounds vague and pretentious, it's because Townshend, not surprisingly, could not hone down the hugely over-ambitious concept into a storyline as he did while creating *Tommy*.

The concept did progress as far as filming the Who and a select audience over a few weeks at London's Young Vic Theatre, while the label of the American single of 'Won't Get Fooled Again' carried the note, 'From the motion picture *Lifehouse*'. Perhaps Pete's lack of time to hammer out a workable plot, the absence of Kit Lambert to exchange ideas, or the sheer impracticality of the basic idea doomed *Lifehouse*. In any event, the Who salvaged several

tracks from a planned double soundtrack album for release on *Who's Next*.

In the midst of the *Lifehouse* developments came the release of *Woodstock* in the summer of 1970. The Who had been disappointed in their performance and their appearance in the film is all too brief, but the finale from *Tommy* is rock at its most powerful. The Who continued to perform *Tommy* even after the intended 'final' performance in June 1970 at the New York Metropolitan Opera House, and thus kept the music and the concept in the public's mind. Behind the scenes, however, it had become bogged down as a film project; Townshend recalls meeting various film producers who all seemed to lack any ideas for the project or proposed only to mime something to the Who's version.

Largely through the efforts of Robert Stigwood, the Who finally teamed up with Ken Russell in 1974. In a *Christian Science Monitor* interview, Russell claimed he never liked the Who's rock version, but was attracted to the idea of a modern Messiah, and felt that *Tommy* continued a theme he had explored in 1972's *Savage Messiah*. Drawing on such acting talent as Ann-Margret, Oliver Reed and Jack Nicholson and casting Daltrey in the title role, Russell stamped his forceful personality and outlandish vision on the film version – notably making blatant parallels with the life of Christ. He also changed the basic story by killing the father, rather than the lover, then using the father figure instead of Tommy's self-awareness as the focus for the film's conclusion.

Lisztophenia

If these intrusions and the new soundtrack destroyed much of the rock music intrinsic to the Who's version, at least Russell created an image faithful to the bombastic, overblown tradition of the opera from which *Tommy* was supposedly drawn. The only drawback was that, upon the film's release in March 1975, *Tommy* was nearly six years old: ancient history in terms of popular culture and rock music. The movie also seemed to serve notice that the follow-up rock opera LP, *Quadrophenia* (1973), had failed to move the Who on to new areas.

With the extended life of *Tommy*, the Who's group image began to crack. Regarding the dynamics of the band itself, the press more and more spoke in terms of 'Pete Townshend's Who', and Daltrey had acquired a public image as Tommy himself. The individuals within the group began a series of solo activities while the Who temporarily took a back seat. Daltrey continued his connection with Russell by taking the leading role in *Lisztomania* (1975), but the film fared badly.

The singer's next effort, *The Legacy* (1977), was even more of a failure. But Daltrey had now become interested in the life of John McVicar, the infamous bank robber and escape artist. Daltrey bought the film rights to McVicar's autobiography and eventually starred in the film version,

McVicar (1980). His performance was both direct and powerful, conveying McVicar's fear of being hunted and refusal to knuckle under to authority.

Keith Moon also tried to find an outlet in films. His acting – as a demented nun in Frank Zappa's *200 Motels* (1971), and as drummer D. J. Clover in *That'll Be The Day* (1973) and *Stardust* (1974) – proved him worthy of greater cinematic exposure, yet his only film role thereafter was that of the perverted Uncle Ernie in *Tommy*.

By the mid Seventies, it seemed the power of the Who was lost to film forever, although avid fans were aware of some of the early promo clips or could recall specific TV shows. 19-year-old Jeff Stein was one such fan who had published a pictorial of the 1971 Who tours. He approached the Who with the idea of collecting as many film clips as possible, and then trying to edit them into a cohesive movie. Apparently, Stein's enthusiasm overcame reservations about his inexperience, and he was given approval for the project. The Who co-operated by providing current interviews and performing a special show for Stein to film. The result was released in 1979 as *The Kids Are Alright*.

Who fans, perhaps justifiably, consider it *the* rock movie; there are a few low spots, but in general the film merits repeated viewing. It portrays not just the excitement of the Who but of rock music as a whole, a commendable accomplishment considering that little of the footage was shot with a particular view in mind.

Jeff Stein's film was possible because in 1977 the Who had invested their money in Shepperton Studios – establishing The Who Films – with plans to produce a variety of movies, one of which was based on *Quadrophenia*. Because the Who had given up playing the album on stage relatively quickly after its release, there was little in the way of preconceived public ideas as to how the story should proceed.

With this freedom, a film script should have been easy to complete, but a first effort involving Chris Stamp and writer Nik Cohn got nowhere. Bill Curbishley stepped in, engaging Roy Baird as scriptwriter and Franc Roddam as director, and the resulting film was a straightforward account of life as a Mod in 1965 London. The Who's music was used only as soundtrack material, while the Who themselves appear only in a short segment from an old TV clip. Despite this, *Quadrophenia* is a Who movie in that it recreates the era during which the High Numbers became the Who.

Rock'n'roll has always involved a little more than just music, and the Who have been masters of creating both good music and a compelling image. The only regret is that far too much of the Who's theatrics escaped the eye of the camera, and what remains gives only a glimpse of their unacknowledged impact on so much of what is happening in today's video world.

ED HANEL

Legal matters and the faces behind the Who

BY THE MID SIXTIES, the enormous worldwide success of the Beatles had shown the business world that there were potentially vast sums of money to be made from the handling and promotion of pop acts. So it is hardly surprising that the progress of the Who from church-hall to stadium status ran parallel with several controversies surrounding the management and marketing of the group.

In 1963, Roger Daltrey, Pete Townshend and John Entwistle formed part of the Detours, along with drummer Doug Sandom, and were playing regularly around the Shepherd's Bush area of London. The group soon acquired a management deal, under which responsibilities were shared by Helmut Gorden and Bob Druce, as well as a new name – the Who.

Druce was a local agent and promoter whose company, Commercial Entertainments Ltd, was able to secure his groups work in a small-time circuit of local halls and clubs. Gorden, on the other hand, had no previous experience within the music business – he was a middle-aged owner of a doorknobs factory – and his bizarre ideas for the Who soon began to irritate the various group members. Gorden did, however, manage to secure an audition with Philips Records, as well as the services of freelance publicist Peter Meaden.

New action
Meaden used an advance from Gorden to buy new clothes for the group, to have their hair restyled and to introduce the Who to Soho's Scene Club, a popular haunt of top Mods. The Who took a third name, the High Numbers; a new drummer was found in Keith Moon, after Sandom had proved to be below par; and Meaden assumed the role of manager. Gorden and Druce dropped out.

Although their 'I'm The Face' single flopped, the High Numbers began to attract an ever-growing following. Gigs at the Railway Tavern, Wealdstone and Watford Trade Hall in September 1964 impressed young film-makers Kit Lambert and Chris Stamp, who were looking for a new group to feature in a short.

Years later, Chris Stamp recalled the effect his first sighting of the Who had on him: 'They were extraordinary, very surreal, just right for our purposes.' But the partners' intentions soon changed; they dropped their film idea and took over the High Numbers' management. Lambert approached Meaden and, in giving him the impression that he (Lambert) was a promoter, had the excellence of the group pushed on him by their ever-eager and hyper-enthusiastic manager. Lambert and Stamp auditioned the group the following day and their offer to become joint managers was accepted by the band a week later. Meaden was subsequently paid £500 as a settlement.

Above: Keith Moon chats with Kit Lambert – both died before they got old.

TRACK RECORD

The new managers paid the High Numbers a salary and continued Meaden's Mod fashion ideas. They placed some white labels with EMI, to have them rejected, changed the group's name back to the Who and secured a residency at the Marquee Club, beginning 24 November.

A girl who knew both Lambert and Kinks producer Shel Talmy was the link that brought a record contract. Talmy saw the group live at a church hall in Shepherd's Bush, auditioned them, then independently cut a recording of 'I Can't Explain' which he used to secure a deal. The Who were signed directly to American Decca, receiving a UK release only through its Brunswick outlet.

'Anyway, Anyhow, Anywhere', 'My Generation' and a first album – *My Generation* – followed, but the relationship between the Who and producer Talmy was eroding, while Lambert and Stamp were unhappy with the two Deccas. The US company was inexperienced in rock promotion while the UK outlet gave a low royalty out of which Talmy took a hefty percentage. Atlantic made Lambert a good offer, including a substantial advance; the latter was now necessary as the Who's debts mounted, mainly because of their treatment of their equipment. The fourth Who single, 'Substitute' – bearing the credit: 'A New Action Production' – was thus released in the US on Atlantic's subsidiary Atco, and on Reaction in the UK.

Going round in circles
Reaction was intended as a stop-gap label, set up by the group's agent Robert Stigwood for Who releases only, but subsequently issued records by Cream and other groups. The flip of 'Substitute' was originally 'Circles', then 'Instant Party' – which was simply 'Circles' retitled in an attempt to obscure the fact that a different version of 'Circles' had been recorded with Talmy and set as the follow-up to 'My Generation'. Talmy placed an injunction on the single, claiming it infringed his copyright and that he still held an exclusive right to record the Who. 'Substitute' was hastily withdrawn from sale and reissued with a new flipside, 'Waltz For A Pig'; it was credited to the Who Orchestra, but was actually played by the Graham Bond Organisation as the injunction barred the Who from recording.

Meanwhile Talmy issued the aptly-titled 'A Legal Matter' from the *My Generation* album, backed by the original version of 'Circles', now also titled 'Instant Party'! The injunction was soon lifted, although it was some months before there would be a final settlement (during which time Talmy continued to release old tracks as each new Who record appeared). The negotiated arrangement gave Talmy a royalty on all Who releases for the next six years, thus including *Tommy*, while Kit Lambert took over as producer.

In April 1967, Lambert and Stamp founded Track Records and the Who's 'Pictures Of Lily' appeared the same month. Track gave the group freedom, but it also laid the foundations of the break which would eventually come between the Who and their managers. For Lambert and Stamp could now no longer be with the group all the time. Road manager John Wolff stepped in as a tour manager, especially necessary as the Who embarked on four separate tours in America that year alone.

Taking the strain

1969's *Tommy* established the Who as an enormously important and successful group, as well as helping to clear the group's debts. Track also proved successful; apart from the Who, the label had acquired the services of the Jimi Hendrix Experience, Arthur Brown and others and was thus taking more and more of Stamp and Lambert's time. Peter Rudge, who had joined Track in 1968 to book tours for Arthur Brown, consolidated himself as the Who's personal manager in all but name. He was responsible for negotiating and arranging tours to promote *Tommy* and in the early Seventies he moved to New York to form SIR Productions to handle the Who's US tours from there. His place in Britain was taken by Bill Curbishley, a friend of Chris Stamp who had also worked his way up through the Track hierarchy.

The 1969 single 'The Seeker' brought other outward signs of the strained relationship. It was produced not by Lambert but by the Who themselves, and in 1971 the *Who's Next* album was produced by Glyn Johns. By mid 1973, Lambert and Stamp had ceased to be managers in any real sense, although they were still drawing considerable royalties from their 1964 agreement with the group.

Nearly two years of legal wrangling followed until an out-of-court settlement was reached in mid 1975. The Who left Track, subsequent releases appearing on Polydor, beginning with *The Who By Numbers* (1975). The Who were now officially managed by Curbishley, with Rudge retained as the US overseer. Chris Stamp meanwhile moved out of music and back to film work, but Lambert, bitter at never receiving the credit he felt due to him for *Tommy*, embarked on a life of excess which came to a sad end when he died after a fall at his mother's home in April 1981. Meanwhile, Track Records had folded in 1978.

Problems and prosperity

In 1976, Rudge pulled out of his relationship in amicable fashion to concentrate on other groups, including the Rolling Stones and Lynyrd Skynyrd, and left Curbishley as the exclusive manager. Curbishley also helped with Peter Meaden's management of the Steve Gibbons Band. Since his split with the Who, Meaden had managed Jimmy James and the Vagabonds and become involved in further publicity work, before collapsing into a world of drugs and

Below: Pete Meaden (centre) with Townshend and Steve Gibbons, 1976.
Bottom: Bill Curbishley picks Roger Daltrey's pocket.

mental problems. He returned to the Who camp in time to help advise on aspects of the *Quadrophenia* film, but his renewed involvement ended with his death in July 1978: an open verdict was recorded.

The Seventies came to a close with a further tragic death within the Who camp – that of Keith Moon – and the ending of the group's long, and initially frustrating, relationship with US Decca. They subsequently signed with Warner Brothers in the States, remaining on Polydor elsewhere (though they later signed to MCA). While many figures instrumental in shaping the Who's destiny had fallen by the wayside, the remaining group members continued to prosper.   BRIAN HOGG

THE SEEKER

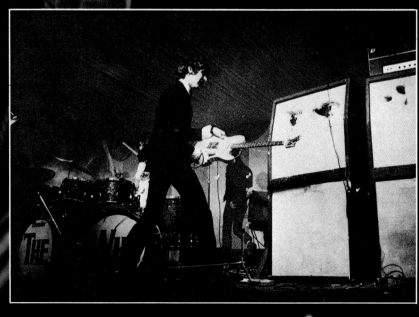

Pete Townshend: from destruction to devotion

PETE TOWNSHEND has spent more than half his life in a seemingly obsessive quest for the truth of rock'n'roll. He has been consistently aware of the contradictions inherent in rock music – full-blown hedonism versus a sense of responsibility – and has continued to thrust these contradictions before the public via a notable series of self-lacerating interviews. 'Forget about the tired old myth that rock'n'roll is just making records, pulling birds, getting pissed and having a good time,' he once said. 'That's not what it's all about. The definition of rock'n'roll lies here for me: if it screams for truth rather than help, if it commits itself with a courage that it can't be sure it really has, if it stands up and admits something is wrong but doesn't insist on blood, then it is rock'n'roll.'

Townshend has never allowed his opinions or emotions to be laundered through rock music's great PR machine, and his sanity and integrity as a rock'n'roll commentator have thus been assured.

Art and machines

Like many pop stars of the Sixties, Pete Townshend attended art school, but – unlike most – he did not devote the duration of his stay to practising blues licks in the toilets. Although music and marijuana were important and exciting elements of art-school life, Townshend was equally influenced by more strictly curricular activities.

At the period when Townshend was in attendance, Ealing Art School had fallen under the influence of a revolutionary new regime, spearheaded by head tutor Roy Ascot. The gospel of the new movement was an art/science called cybernetics, which is defined as the study of automatic communication and control in living bodies and mechanical systems; Townshend pounced upon the possibilities that the cross-fertilisation of art and machines might offer, first in visual terms, then – more significantly – in audio-visual terms. The systematic man/machine violence of the early Who set was a crude example of performance art: such intellectual rage has characterised Townshend throughout his career. 'I smash guitars because I like them,' he once stated. 'I usually smash a guitar when it's at its best. I don't have a love affair with a guitar – I don't polish it after every performance. I play the damned thing.' Townshend both embodied and debunked the myth of the guitar hero almost before it had been formulated.

Another vital element in Townshend's rock'n'roll apprenticeship was the enigmatic figure of Andy 'Thunderclap' Newman, a post office engineer who made experimental music in his spare time. One lunch hour, Newman turned up at Ealing Art School to give his first-ever public performance, and played a series of bizarre numbers to the accompaniment of piano,

kazoo and metronome. Townshend was immensely impressed and was subsequently introduced to the strange 'genius'. (Years later, in 1969, Townshend helped to form a group around Newman, called simply Thunderclap Newman, and produced their first single, 'Something In The Air', which reached Number 1 in the UK.)

It was not so much Newman's music as his methods which were to influence Townshend. Newman had begun experimenting with tape recorders at a very early stage and had developed quite sophisticated multi-tracking techniques. 'Before I even knew what tape recording was, he was into it,' Townshend later recalled. 'Multi-tracking bird songs and locomotive recordings – special effects, echoes . . .' Through Newman, Townshend came to recognise the potential of the tape recorder, both as a means to achieving a vast range of effects and, more importantly, an instrument which facilitated the process of writing music. In those days, groups crammed in as many live dates as

Above: Townshend tinkers with tape. A fascination with multi-tracking helped his composing abilities in the Who's early days. Opposite: Spectacular leaps and battered guitars – hallmarks of Pete Townshend's energetic performances.

possible and, if luck and finance permitted, were rushed into a studio to record a couple of songs in an hour by means of a process of which they were almost entirely ignorant. The benefit of Townshend's home taping was that it gave him the opportunity to try out ideas and to understand how the best way of presenting them might be achieved.

The public's perception of Townshend as a demented wrecker at the time of the Who's early success was, therefore, somewhat less than the complete picture – the basis of both the live act and the sound of the early singles was the result of some very shrewd assimilation by Pete Town-

shend. Then Kit Lambert made his appearance. The Who had already undergone a crash course in pills, looks, sounds and all things Mod from Pete Meaden, who handled publicity for the group for a short time, and typically it was Townshend who soaked up this new influence. It was Lambert, however, who exercised the greatest influence of all. He instantly singled out Townshend as the creative force within the Who and lavished attention upon him. This attention ranged from introducing Townshend to fine wines and the best restaurants to exposing him to classical and baroque music for the first time – 'I think the first manifestation of Kit's influence was on the song 'The Kids Are Alright' where I actually started to use baroque chords, suspended chords. It did a lot to create that churchy feel and had a lot to do with the way I play.' As well as providing a specific musical influence, the operatic music Townshend was listening to also suggested a wider context for pop songs. By their second album, *A Quick One*, the Who were playing around with a 'mini-opera' and *Tommy* was only a short step away.

Baba O'Riley

Shortly after the monstrous success of *Tommy*, however, Lambert was to all intents and purposes ousted as the group's adviser/producer and the Who – or, rather, Pete Townshend – were left to their own devices to fashion a follow-up project. But Townshend was now finding ideas hard to pin down. In mid 1968 he had become a follower of Eastern guru Meher Baba, and the lack of spiritual discipline and the emphasis on the individual which Baba's teachings promoted were not making writing easy: 'I'm still on a kind of self with a capital S trip. It's a bit difficult, writing heavy when you really want to write light,' Townshend confessed at the time. Nowhere was this more apparent than in the *Lifehouse* fiasco. This overloaded rock parable was of breathtaking obscurity and at one mad moment it was to involve the Who living with 2000 fans in London's Young Vic theatre for six months. Looking back on it, Pete commented: 'I'd spend a week explaining something to somebody and it'd be all very clear to me, then they'd go, "Right, okay, now can you explain it again?" Everybody was treating me as if I was some kind of loony and I think for a while I lost touch with reality.'

Much of the *Lifehouse* trauma was exorcised by *Who's Next* (a track from which, 'Baba O'Riley', was in part dedicated to the avant-garde musician Terry Riley, indicating that Townshend remained receptive to all types of material) but the major work, and one that encapsulated much of the Townshend philosophy, was *Quadrophenia*. A later comment by Pete is revealing: 'I'm no punk any more, if I ever was. I always stood outside looking in, and always will.' It is this gift of passionate objectivity that has characterised Townshend's most inspired writing from the time of 'My Generation', while his solo albums, beginning with the revealingly entitled *Who Came First?* in 1972, represent something of a commentary on his main output with the Who.

Empty glass

The songs on Townshend's solo albums tend towards introspective or devotional themes and in a number like 'I Am An Animal' (from the *Empty Glass* LP of 1980) Townshend dissects himself for public inspection in a manner completely alien to the conventions of rock superstardom. Townshend is unique in his constant urge to own up – to rows with Roger Daltrey, bouts of drinking and drug-taking, to marital infidelity.

The ultimate owning-up was reserved for the British punk explosion. 1975 had begun with a series of Townshend tirades in the press against the dire state of rock in general and Daltrey in particular. As if in answer to a prayer, the Sex Pistols lurched into view the following year and Pete com-

Below: A 1981 Amnesty International benefit saw Townshend appear with Japan's Mick Karn (left) and Ultravox's Midge Ure. Right: Face of the future? Townshend's 1982 solo LP.

mented, 'In my imagination I invented punk rock a thousand times.' During an evening at the Speakeasy club, Pete met Steve Jones and Paul Cook of the Pistols and harangued them about the need to pick up rock's fallen banner and carry it proudly forward. 'What does it matter if the Who break up? We're destroyed. We've compromised everything to bits. We're prostitutes.' Yet somehow there is always a regeneration of energy and ideas. 'You know something – I really hate feeling too old to be doing what I'm doing' is a typical

Townshend comment, but his responsibility to his chosen art is such as to preclude a premature exit.

1982's *All The Best Cowboys Have Chinese Eyes* confirmed the promise of *Empty Glass*, with a collection of intensely personal songs alongside a radical reworking of the traditional 'North Country Girl'. As with its predecessor, the album eschewed the all-too-frequent 'superstar with heavy friends' solo project format in favour of a solid rhythm section (Tony Butler and Mark Brzezicki, formerly of brother Simon's band and later of Big Country) and thoughtful arrangements. Later activities included releasing two albums of demos, *Scoop* and *Another Scoop*, a concept album/video in 1985's *White City* and an occasional band, Deep End, with Pink Floyd's Dave Gilmour.

Honesty of the Townshend variety is rare in the rock world both in what is accomplished and in how it regards itself. Few others could sum themselves up like this: 'I'm very heavily into Meher Baba, but I also drink like a fish. I'm still not the most honest person in the world. It's difficult, but I do at least know what's happening to me. I accept that there is a larger reason for me being alive than just being a rock star.'   PETER CLARK

Sound and Vision

Artists, photographers, designers and the visual element in rock

ROCK IS NOT ONLY MUSIC – it is also visual impact. It is *sight* and sound. The look of a group or singer can be crucial in ensuring success; however well they can play, they will find it very difficult to make an impact on a young mass market unless they dress the part.

This truism – that it is not only what you play, but what you look like when you're doing it – has held good from the earliest days of rock to the present. Sam Phillips' search for the white boy who sang black; Jack Good bedecking Gene Vincent in leather; Brian Epstein persuading the Beatles to smarten up; the swing of fashion from flowers and long hair in the late Sixties to the extremes of punk clothing in the late Seventies were all part of the same phenomenon.

It is fairly clear how and why this phenomenon works. Rock is not mere art music for consumption and disposal. For its predominantly youthful audience, it expresses their unspoken emotions, gives them goals to dream about and images to copy. In a general sense, the way you look is perhaps the most important means of expressing identity, and for a youthful audience it can proclaim both independence from one's parents and the need to belong – either to one's own generation or to some self-contained sub-group within it.

Pin-up posers

From this basis there are, of course, any number of offshoots that give the visual image even more power – the need for some teenage girls to idolise young men who are sexual but not sexually threatening, for example. There are also certain constants in popular music that reinforce this; conventionally attractive singers (of either sex) tend to do better than ugly ones.

It is the complications in these areas that make visual image such an ambivalent area in rock. It can seem very natural – a precise counterpoint to the music in the Small Faces embodying the dress sense of their audience, or the Clash looking the part they played – but it can also be the most cynical manipulation of mass emotions. The three examples quoted earlier – Sam Phillips and Elvis, Jack Good and Gene Vincent, Brian Epstein and the Beatles – are all about creating a recognisable image to sell. In the early Seventies, in 'teenybop' groups, the process seemed to go even further, and it would be hard to condone the methods of some managers and record companies in producing puppets who looked right but could barely play. There were several famous cases of session musicians being brought in to supply the sound to suit the others' look.

But whatever the complications of this relationship between music and image, it is undeniable that rock's concern with visual impact and style has had great effects in all areas it has touched. The record sleeve was turned into an art form by rock; painting could not help but be affected by the sheer visual excitement of the new music; and photography – the most important of the methods by which rock stars were 'seen' by their audience (outside live performance) – was given whole new frontiers to cross.   ASHLEY BROWN

Studio photography assumed an increasing importance in rock with the growing image-consciousness of bands in the late Seventies. Japan (below) continually evolved their image to outlast the popular, yet short-lived, new romantic movement.

PICTURE THIS..

Snap decisions: the art of rock photography

ROCK PHOTOGRAPHY is about rock musicians and their music and about photography. There are two main types of picture – portraits (non-performing) and stage shots; whether or not the music can ever be encapsulated in a visual image, rock as live performance and skilful playing lends itself brilliantly to dramatic, colourful and dynamic stage shots – capturing the excitement, atmosphere, lights, the style of the performer and what they are getting across to the audience.

Styles and fashions in photographs are set by a very few photographers and designers, and are therefore slow to change. The music press is an important forum for the influence of new ideas to reach the music business in general, but the highly conservative rock business is slow to accept newcomers and even slower to acknowledge their worth. Hence many potential candidates are lured away by the financial rewards of other areas of photography. Most people who get into rock photography do so out of love for the music and a desire to be in some way involved in 'the business'. The peculiar thing about the rock world is the transitory nature of most of it. Today's photo session is forgotten tomorrow if the group depicted fails to make an impact. Fads and fashions in music change so fast that it is a constant race to keep up.

Publicity shots are essential to all show-business. In rock, the record companies and the powerful photographic agencies that feed the national press with studio-shot publicity photographs are the main arbiters of taste in this field. Photographers here have the group's full co-operation and the financial support of agency syndication, but the conservatism in style is strong, being dictated by the limitations of national newspaper layout requirements. Also the agency cannot sell off-the-wall pictures to a mass market, no matter how much the artist or group might think such photography relevant.

Live pictures can be purely artistic; but they are also geared towards publicity, like studio portrait shots taken to project a particular image – rock is, after all, extremely commercial and photographs play their part in the money-spinning process.

The single most important influence on rock photography since its identifiable origins in the Fifties has undoubtedly been of a technical nature: the cameras, films and printing-reproduction techniques. The

From the early record company promotion shots (the Contours, top right) to Eighties sophistication (Classix Nouveaux, top far right), studio photography has changed little in its basic purpose – to project the right image. The Beatles (left) are made to look clean-cut, while carefully arranged background and lighting lend a sense of menace to the Clash (right).

undesirable colour. Flash photography was therefore the norm, producing flat, rather static-looking pictures lacking in both quantity and variety.

In the Seventies all this changed. The advent of quartz and high-intensity tungsten halogen lamps increased the brightness tenfold and the consistency of light quality of spotlights improved to daylight comparability. By the end of the Seventies quite complex and impressive lighting rigs were being used even in small clubs. As a result, managements and groups soon began actively discouraging unauthorised photographers, not because of the individual value of the photographs or a desire to deny the fan a picture, but the fear of the damage to the image and carefully-controlled official merchandising sales.

For the professional, this has meant increasing restrictions both in time to photograph a show (commonly limited to the first three numbers only) and in the subsequent use of the pictures that are taken. Artists will often insist on quite complex contracts being signed prior to issuing the essential authorisation. These may restrict the use of pictures to just one nominated publication – and the artist can still insist on approval of the pictures before they are used. Even with the artists' authorisation, access to front-of-stage can still be thwarted by safety regulations.

After official permission to photograph a concert has been gained, other problems arise. The stage might be too high, too low or have no 'photo pit' or security barrier in front. A high stage requires photography from a long way back, necessitating the use of long telephoto lenses and presenting difficulties; these are not just technical, in terms of holding the camera still enough to obtain a sharp image, but also of perspective. Shooting from a distance is very acceptable for a whole-stage shot that gives each musician equal prominence, and for showing off the stage set to best advantage, but otherwise produces flat, undynamic pictures. A low stage presents even greater problems unless there is a photo pit. Trying to work in the front rows of an excited audience is an experience most fans with a little pocket camera have had; it often produces excellent pictures,

lightweight 35mm SLR (single lens reflex) camera has become the standard for press work, while in the Seventies fully-automatic exposure and motor-drive cameras became quite commonplace. Colour and (to a lesser degree) black-and-white film has undergone several dramatic improvements in quality and ease of use during the same period. These advances in photography coincided with an equally spectacular advance in stage presentation and lighting systems, and an increased awareness of the potential of live photographs.

In the Fifties and Sixties, lighting was for the most part rudimentary, consisting

of a carbon arc spotlight or two and some low-intensity stage colour washes of the kind used in theatrical productions. This was fine for viewing but useless for photography – not just because of the low light level, but because the main 'white light' spotlight was likely to be recorded by the colour film as a sickly green or another

Lighting has affected stage photography since the days of Chuck Berry (above), when flashlight was needed, through the more powerful early Seventies rigs of bands like Led Zeppelin (below left) to Queen (below right) with their elaborate stage effects.

A wide-angle lens was necessary to fit in the
full width of the stage at this AC/DC concert
(above). At another venue (below) the best
camera angle was from the wings.

but looking after two cameras, eight lenses and a bag full of film in such conditions can pose problems.

A photo pit to work in isn't always ideal, however, even if the stage is at eye level or lower. The front edge of the stage is usually cluttered with monitor speakers arranged for the convenience of the musicians to hear themselves, and these can assume gigantic stage-filling proportions viewed from close proximity. Even in the biggest lighting rigs, only a small number of lamps will actually be useful at any one moment, and the main spotlights will often beam a strong primary colour that does not come out too well in print – red, for example. Of course the different colours produced by stage lighting add to the interest in the pictures, but that depends entirely on who is buying the shots. Such considerations are secondary to getting a good, sharp, well-composed, well-lit picture. Often quite simple lighting rigs give best results because the light is better positioned, closer to the musician and therefore consistently brighter.

It is the capturing of rock's strong visual impact in live performance that gives rock photography an identity of its own. Modern rock photography with its emphasis on available light and candid styles dates from the late Sixties, and the emergence of progressive rock in 1968 produced groups who benefit from this approach, specifically groups with a front man for visual appeal, such as the Who and Led Zeppelin. During the boom years of the early Seventies, many such British bands gained international success and helped give the rock photographer both a steady market and a defined role.

Image and imagination
The designs and possibilities of light on stage and in photographic studios are now greater than ever, and play a significant part in the image-building process; and the employment of modern studio techniques has produced a marked improvement in the quality of publicity photographs through the years. Many groups take on the services of one photographer to the exclusion of all others; this effectively fixes a chosen look produced in collaboration with that photographer and sets an image that is zealously guarded. Other types of non-performing shot are not particularly related to rock. The candid/documentary pictures of the artists that are probably the most fascinating to fans can sometimes be merely snapshots. In the hands of a talented photographer, however, who knows and is trusted by the artist, such pictures can become the most artistically

Above left: A full-stage shot of Bob Dylan and band, taken from the audience. Left: The use of a telephoto lens from the same spot allows a close-up, but the picture lacks depth and perspective. Right: A pit in front of the stage here provides the location for an uncluttered, dramatic photograph of T. Rex's Marc Bolan.

worthy, too. They also give a true feel of the era to which the artist belongs.

As much as anything else, rock is also about creators of music and lyrics, and therefore lends itself to moody, individual photographs designed to capture the character of the artist rather than (or as well as) a public image. Often the best medium for this type of picture is black and white, and much of the value of the photo lies in the photographer's creative skill; this can include his eye for the right composition, care in producing the print itself with correct contrast and cropping to produce the desired effect.

Although some artists are perhaps better represented in this way – particularly singer-songwriters such as Simon and Garfunkel who are not dynamic on stage – this kind of picture has more to do with portrait photography than rock. But whatever the required approach, rock performers of all types continue to inspire photographers to ever higher levels of artistry – providing them with a constant challenge as rock images and styles change. ROBERT ELLIS

Mood shots – from an ingenuous early snap of three Beatles (below) to this powerful portrait of Burning Spear (left) – have always been popular.

ART ON THEIR SLEEVES

stereo

with the beatles

PARLOPHONE

THE COMING OF AGE of the record sleeve can be pinpointed as occurring in 1963 with the release of the Beatles' second album, *With The Beatles*. The photograph on the group's first album, *Please Please Me*, had shown a bunch of cheerful rock'n'rollers (Ringo even had the memory of a quiff) gazing down from the balcony of EMI's Manchester Square headquarters; *With The Beatles*, however, bore a high-contrast black-and-white 'portrait' by fashion photographer Robert Freeman. The first sleeve was sales-conscious (as its title and the legend "With 'Love Me Do'" testified), the second was an attempt at art.

Equally significantly, this landmark in the history of sleeve design came at a time when the popular arts, and especially the technology-oriented ones – photography, the cinema and music – and the people involved, be they fashion models or pop

How the rock album was dressed to sell

stars, were collectively forming Swinging London. Suddenly pop wasn't looked down on and accordingly the design of its product, the album, could be taken seriously by artists and designers who were in sympathy with the music. Thus *With The Beatles* wasn't unique for long: a year later another fashion photographer, David Bailey, paid Freeman the compliment of imitating his cover – substituting menace for the Beatles' enigmatic presence – on the Rolling Stones' second LP.

Strong image, stark black and white – the classic With The Beatles *sleeve (above left). In contrast, the Grateful Dead's* American Beauty *(above right) had a folksy wrapper.*

Soundtracks on 78

With the exception of a few scattered jazz sleeves and iconographically resonant rock'n'roll sleeves (such as Elvis' first album, *Elvis Presley*, which has a naivety and unselfconsciousness about it that remains powerful to this day), record sleeves of the Fifties and earlier were rarely 'designed' as such. Indeed, at the turn of the century, when the flat record replaced the cylinder, records were not even protected by paper – let alone cardboard – sleeves. And when it became common practice to give records sleeves, it wasn't the record companies but the retailers, worried about breakages, who introduced the cardboard sleeves that quickly became synonymous with the 78 rpm record.

It was only with the advent of the album book (a collection of 78s in a box) in the early Forties that the advertisements for

As rock album sleeve design has become more self-conscious, designers have often taken past designs as a reference point. Sometimes the allusion is indirect – the typography of many of Elvis Costello's covers suggests the jazz era – but occasionally whole designs are plagiarised almost intact. Cartoonist Ray Lowry borrowed the design of Elvis Presley's first LP (below) and, combin-

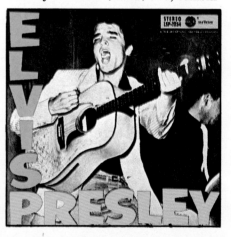

phonograph needles, the retailers themselves or bland catalogue lists were replaced by a colour portrait or drawing of the artist in question. The dominant influence, as one would expect, was the cinema, whose soundtracks gave the record companies many of their first album books and whose posters and star portraits were easily adapted by the companies for their sleeves. The message was the brash, vulgar one that Hollywood was best known for: buy, buy, buy.

In contrast to this, the significant thing about the design of jazz sleeves of the Fifties and early Sixties, especially those of small companies like Blue Note, was that an attempt was made to visualise the music for its intended audience. It was this, transferred to the mass market, that made the revolution that followed *With The Beatles* so important.

Top left: Classic English psychedelia – Cream's Disraeli Gears. *Left: The glowing Wild West romanticism of Quicksilver Messenger Service's* Happy Trails *LP.*

ing it with another piece of classic symbolism, the guitar hero trashing his axe, applied it to the Clash's *London Calling* (below). The cover of Elvis Costello's *Almost Blue* (above) bears the same relationship to that of Kenny Burrell's *Midnight Blue* (above left), a ploy that complements the conscious revivalism of Costello's country-and-western-flavoured album.

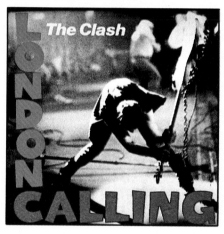

Accordingly, when the album replaced the single as the music's major means of communication and rock superseded pop to become the centre of the counter-culture that emerged in the mid Sixties, record sleeves quickly became as essential a component of that culture as psychedelic posters and tie-dye grandad vests. This new-found importance of the sleeve as well as the music was reflected in several ways. Following the lead of the Beatles, who commissioned Peter Blake to design the sleeve of 1967's *Sgt Pepper's Lonely Hearts Club Band* and Richard Hamilton to design the 'White Album', other artists demanded a say in the presentation of their work to the public, just as they were demanding greater freedom in the recording studio. Thus, record sleeves quickly came to suggest and describe what music was inside.

In some cases, they became yet another

The bold, garish sleeve for the Psychedelic Sounds Of The 13th Floor Elevators *(top right) contrasted with the more cerebral experiments of Victor Moscoso (right).*

It's in the can – the Small Faces LP Ogden's Nut Gone Flake came in a lovingly reproduced tobacco tin that opened up to reveal a pack of cigarette papers. The only snag – it kept rolling off the shelf.

battleground between artists and their more conservative masters. The Rolling Stones' planned cover for *Beggars Banquet* (1968), which was to show a graffiti-covered toilet wall, was banned by Decca, while the Beatles' original cover for their American compilation *Yesterday And Today* (1966), which showed the group in butchers' aprons holding dismembered dolls and chunks of bloody meat as a protest against the Vietnam War, was pasted over with a bland publicity shot.

The power of the companies' design departments was challenged at the same time by the arrival of artist-oriented design studios like Hipgnosis in England and Globe Propaganda (among others) in San Francisco, which transferred the concerns of psychedelia from poster to sleeve. Moreover, since the companies found albums far more profitable than singles, they were willing to spend more on them. One way was to give more time and resources to a designer; another, especially after the arrival of the gatefold sleeve, was to give him more space. Thus, the mid Sixties saw a spectacular explosion in the art of sleeve design that was marked above all by a willingness to confront the public and give a flavour of the music inside, rather than merely promote the product.

Dayglo daydream
Of the purely psychedelic sleeves, the cover of the 13th Floor Elevators' first album, *Psychedelic Sounds Of The 13th Floor Elevators* (1967), was the most direct. Like the music of this Texan group, the

sleeve offered a brash version of psychedelia that could only be carried off at a considerable distance from the source of inspiration, San Francisco. In comparison, the lurid colour games devised by SF psychedelic artist Victor Moscoso for the cover of Steve Cropper's *With A Little Help From My Friends* (1971) seemed tame, almost classical. Cream's *Disraeli Gears* (1967) offered a dayglo daydream version

of psychedelia – less forceful, more evocative, more British, but equally successful.

But psychedelic music did not only produce psychedelic covers. An important strand in the San Francisco scene was nostalgia. This was best captured by George Hunter in a series of sleeves which constituted an art form in their own right. His covers for Quicksilver Messenger Service's *Happy Trails* (1969) and It's A Beautiful Day's eponymous debut (1969) conveyed romanticism and strong echoes of the 'innocent' nineteenth-century cowboy artists. Kelly's cover for the Grateful Dead's *American Beauty* (1970) was similar in feel, but more elaborately (yet 'invisibly') staged. Looking like a 'found object', it spoke of craftsmanship (much valued by hippies) and perfectly caught the mood of the music inside.

Below left and below: The Four Seasons adopt the ever-popular newspaper format. Other artists to hold the front page were John Lennon, Jethro Tull and PiL.

Nostalgia – this time for an artefact of British working-class culture, a tobacco tin – lay behind the sleeve design of the Small Faces' *Ogden's Nut Gone Flake* (1968), the best of the gimmick sleeves that abounded from the late Sixties on. Records then masqueraded as anything from greetings cards (such as Tim Buckley's 1972 album *Greetings From LA*, which wittily used the message side to list the tracks) to cigarette lighters (the Wailers' *Catch A Fire*).

The use of gimmicks, however, wasn't confined to good records. Only too often the design studio was called in to rescue disasters created in the recording studio. Two classic examples of this are the Four Seasons' *Genuine Imitation Life Gazette* (1968), which came complete with its own newspaper (a favoured object of sleeve designers) and the Guess Who's *Artificial Paradise* (1974), which parodied the special-offer come-on letter so wonderfully. In both cases the records failed to live up to their packaging.

A more modest and thoughtful use of packaging was Loring Eutemey's series of covers for Atlantic and its related labels. The company had been very successful with soul in the mid Sixties, selling to whites as well as blacks, and wanted to consolidate its position. Thus for the first time soul albums were aimed at whites and their covers given an upmarket look. Atlantic were fortunate to choose Eutemey who, over a series of covers, established a witty look that gave soul a respectability and a strong visual identity. Thus in contrast to the naivety of Bobby Bland's *Call On Me* (the charming literalism of its images notwithstanding), the cover of Albert King's *Born Under A Bad Sign* had a wit and confidence that would make a browser stop when he or she reached it in the racks.

The unconscious drama of the cover of *Call On Me* reaches its conscious climax in the gnomic cover of Dylan's 1968 LP *John Wesley Harding*, which had people turning it this way and that, especially after

Sleeve images have moved from naive literalism (below), through confident allusion (below right) to the puzzles of John Wesley Harding *(below far right).*

Though it usually bears little relation to the product being sold, sex sells: a scantily-clad model is an uninspired and cheap – if successful – marketing technique. The public have become brainwashed by advertisers into buying the product because of a female form draped across a car bonnet or album cover. Some sleeves, like that of Whitesnake's *Lovehunter* (right), flaunt flesh for a basic, crude appeal, while others, like that of the first Roxy Music LP (above), clothe it in arty eroticism; but both methods beg the question, 'What does this image tell you about the band and their music?' Whitesnake blatantly court a particular market with an image of machismo and sexual prowess; Roxy Music do it more 'tastefully', but the ultimate effect is the same. Both records offer the fantasy of escape from

humdrum reality, into a world of elegance and style with Roxy or one of mythical grandeur with Whitesnake, and both promise power over women.

Dylanologists claimed to see faces in the trees that, like the sleeve note, might be the key to the album's hidden meaning.

The hard sell
This sense of freedom and experimentation ended in the mid Seventies when, after the first signs of recession, the companies cut back on album costs and started demanding covers that *sold* rather than merely illustrated. It was from this time that interviews with industry figures brought forth dogmatic assertions that the artist and title must figure in the top third of the sleeve, this being the only portion visible in the racks. The net effect of this retrenchment was to make even more visible the power of bands like Pink Floyd, still being served by Hipgnosis who, a decade on, had established themselves as a major design studio. *Dark Side Of The Moon*, with its cool geometric minimalism and its suggestion of deep meaning, caught the feel of the Floyd's album perfectly, and the

Seventies gatefolds – Yes's Tales From Topographic Oceans *(above)*; Pink Floyd's Dark Side Of The Moon *(above right)*.

Variations on a theme: picture discs *(right)*, punk graphics *(below right)* and the social realism of a UB40 card *(bottom right)*.

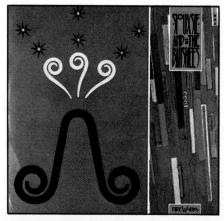

Designers seeking to achieve a specific effect or conjure a particular atmosphere through a knowing use of visual reference have drawn not only on the traditions of sleeve artwork, but on outside sources from graphic and fine arts. Malcolm Garrett's design for the cover of Magazine's LP *The Correct Use Of Soap* (above) utilises the bold, angular figurations of Russian Revolutionary Constructivists like Lazar El Lissitzky (below). A more opulent, *fin de siècle* effect has been achieved by Rocking Russian's borrowing of Viennese artist Gustav Klimt's characteristic gold blocking (left) for the cover of Siouxsie and the Banshees' 12-inch single, 'Fireworks' (above left). Both covers effectively echo the character of the music on the records.

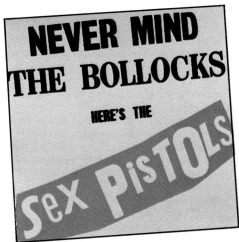

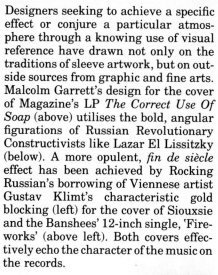

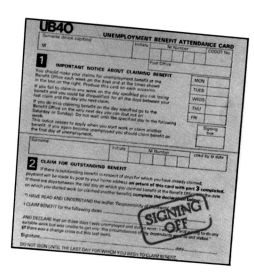

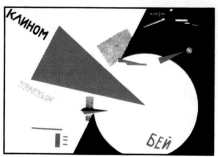

absence of the band's name from the cover flaunted their status; they were so big that it wasn't necessary. (Led Zeppelin did the same on their fourth album, which only had four Icelandic runes as a title.) Similarly, Roger Dean's magical landscapes gave the Yes albums an identity that some critics thought was stronger than the music on them. But they were the exceptions. For the most part record sleeves of the mid Seventies onwards reflected a real confusion felt by artists and designers as they plundered the warehouse of styles in an indiscriminate manner that quickly led to overkill. Fittingly, this period ended with the ultimate gimmick – the picture disc, which embedded the cover artwork in a transparent vinyl disc at the expense of the sound quality.

The same urge to collect that inspired the picture disc prompted Seventies independents like Stiff Records to try to make every single collectable. This policy led to a number of witty sleeves, of which the one for Madness' first album and Ian Dury's *Do It Yourself*, which came in a choice of 10 wallpaper patterns, were classic examples. But it was punk that marked the return to confidence of sleeve designers. The dayglo colours of *Disraeli Gears* were dreamlike: on *Never Mind The Bollocks* they conjured up the vomit that many journalists associated with the anarchic ways of the Sex Pistols. The result was a cover that spoke volumes through simplicity and the use of a strong image. A similar cover was that for UB40's first album, with its literal use of the unemployment benefit card that gave the band its name and signalled their preoccupation with social concerns. Twenty years on from *Please Please Me*, it is clear that record sleeves are approached with a style and sophistication that makes a trip to the record shop more and more like a jaunt to a contemporary art gallery.

PHIL HARDY

Album sleeves have come to visualise not only the music but the musicians' image of themselves. The cover of Pink Floyd's *Ummagumma* (above), with its mirror games, elegant lawns and carefully arranged artefacts (including the soundtrack LP from the musical *Gigi*), creates an impression of self-conscious, intellectual 'cool'; the Floyd later preferred anonymity and kept their own faces off their album sleeves. The photo on the sleeve of Patti Smith's *Horses* (below), in stark black and white, presents an image of hip, androgynous chic. Both covers sell the records inside by offering the buyer a passport to social and intellectual credibility; sleeves to leave, casually strewn, on a coffee table to impress one's friends.

Below: Released in 1974, the Guess Who's Artificial Paradise *LP came wrapped in an artful, elaborately produced parody of a direct mail advertising circular.*

Pop Goes The Easel

When art went pop and rock went art

In 1964 a series of images of Elvis Presley emerged from Warhol's New York art factory – larger than life-size, harshly coloured and brashly aggressive. Part of a production line of Liz Taylors, Jackie Kennedys and Marilyn Monroes, the Elvis images were about fame and superstardom. They required no comment from Warhol or external references for their impact and were instantly recognisable. They were not about his music and they were not about Elvis himself. They dealt with his 'ready-made' image as it appeared in countless magazines, TV shows, films, newspapers and fanzines. At the same time, but in England, David Oxtoby was also exhibiting pictures of rock musicians. His interest lay not in painting portraits of them as such, or the visual impact of their performing presence, but in capturing the essence of their sound and translating its dynamics into painted images on canvas.

Since the late Fifties, rock has forged many connections with the visual arts. Musicians and artists have collaborated on sound and visual projects for live performance. Some, such as Paul Roberts of Sniff 'n' the Tears and Mick Karn of Japan, have worked successfully in both fields. Song lyrics have inspired illustrators, filmmakers and painters, providing them with a mass of visual narratives and lifestyle images from which to draw. Painters have found in rock stars ready-made symbols of both past and present, ranging from moody and sentimental nostalgia for the Fifties to the bleak high-rise anorexia of the late Seventies.

Bringing it all together

Traditionally the relationship between music and the visual arts has always been uneasy. In the Twenties the Dadaists experimented with the fusion of painting, sculpture, music, poetry and theatre at the Cabaret Voltaire, but despite these attempts the lines between such arts remained well-drawn. In the early Fifties, at the Dover Street premises of London's Institute of Contemporary Arts, moves were made by a group of young painters, architects, sculptors and photographers to break out of the rigidity of the established artistic pigeonholes. Regular meetings of the Independent Group, as they were known, explored not only current trends and concerns in the arts but also the many facets of the mid-twentieth-century popular environment of pulp magazines, science-fiction movies, pop music, car design, pin-ups and advertising, most of which was imported from America. From these meetings, British Pop Art was born.

To the artists concerned, among whom

Left: Rock painter David Oxtoby with one panel from his double portrait of Elvis Presley, The King – Fairground Sounds. *The other half depicts the young Elvis.*

were Peter Blake and Richard Hamilton, a whole new area of subject matter was revealed. They felt that their art and their lives could not be separated; and, as avid consumers of popular culture, the everyday images that they saw there soon began to play an important role in their work. In the late Fifties and early Sixties, Blake painted a number of pictures that reflected his interest in rock; *Girls With Their Hero* is a scrapbook-like painting of Elvis pictures derived from magazine photos. The Elvis image reappears in his 1961 *Self-portrait With Buttons*, which shows Blake dressed in denims and holding an Elvis fanzine. *Got A Girl* (1960-61) consists of a large red, white and blue chevron image in the lower half of the picture, while above it Blake has assembled a gallery of teen-idol portraits of Fabian, Frankie Avalon, Bobby Darin and Elvis cut from magazines and pasted onto the surface. A copy of the single 'Got A Girl' – which mentions the pictured artists in its lyric – is attached.

These new ideas were soon to spread among the younger generation of artists experimenting with pop images at the Royal College of Art. Pauline Bothy, who featured in the 1962 Ken Russell TV film 'Pop Goes The Easel', was painting large canvasses of fragmented images of contemporary life. Lenin, Einstein, Cassius Clay and the Kennedy assassination appeared side-by-side with Elvis and the Beatles. Television, advertising and the popular press threw up countless images, and pop music was as much a part of that environment as politics and warfare. Within the art schools themselves rock bands proliferated, musicians such as Keith Richards, Pete Townshend and Syd Barrett starting their careers as art students. To the artists their subject matter was universal – outside of theoretical intellectual concerns – and ready-made and widely available.

Cover versions
By the late Sixties, established artists like Blake and Hamilton were working directly with rock. Blake had painted a portrait of the Beatles that was later to appear as the cover illustration for George Melly's book on the Sixties, *Revolt Into Style*. He had also made the sleeve for the *Sgt Pepper* album. Hamilton was also working with the Beatles, producing the give-away poster and sleeve design for the 'White Album'. Art was coming out of the gallery. John Lennon was writing and drawing, and in the Robert Fraser gallery in London's West End a psychedelically-painted motor car was on exhibition. So was Lennon's painted Rolls, but in the streets. Sci-fi writer J. G. Ballard, friend of the sculptor Eduardo Paolozzi, showed wrecked American cars at the Arts Lab and the floodgates were open for mixed-media.

While in America Warhol was staging the Velvet Underground in his Exploding Plastic Inevitable mixed-media show at the Dom in New York,

Above: Warhol's silkscreen Double Elvis. *Below:* Got A Girl, *by Peter Blake. Bottom: Mick Karn with two of his sculptures.*

rock music and the visual arts were making tentative moves towards each other in the London clubs. Pink Floyd were already using slide projections, flickering films and flashing lights as part of their show in early 1966, and continued to experiment at the UFO and Middle Earth clubs. The 14 Hour Technicolor Dream staged in London in April 1967 included contributions by the painter Barry Fantoni and the 26 Kingly Street group of environmental artists, as well as the manic Crazy World of Arthur Brown, the ubiquitous Floyd and the Soft Machine. The summer of 1967 was also to see Jefferson Airplane at the Roundhouse with their own 'underground' movies showing in the interval.

Throughout the Seventies, Pink Floyd's involvement with the visual arts became steadily more lavish and extravagant. Rockets, dry-ice and airport beacons mixed with the projected images of money, air-

contemporary descriptions that still exist. While the music was captured on record and tape, the images have gone. Those images that have survived belong to the more traditional media of painting and graphics.

While the Pop artists of the Sixties made a great many references to rock music in their paintings, these references were only part of a much broader usage of popular mass-reproduced images. Since the Sixties, however, an increasingly large number of artists have concentrated on rock as subject-matter. One of the best-known of the resulting works was *Rock Dreams*, a collaboration between Nik Cohn, author of the apocalyptic rock novel *I Am The Greatest Says Johnny Angelo*, and illustrator Guy Peellaert, which was published in 1973.

Subtitled 'Under The Boardwalk', the book concerns itself with the underlying obsessions and romance of rock. Hank Williams sprawls dead in the back of a Cadillac, pills scattered across the floor, while the Beach Boys, surrounded by high-school cheerleaders, are followed on the next page by the flashing white teeth and well-filled bikinis of the 'California Girls'. From Dylan to Joe Tex, the pictures and Cohn's captions are cutting and filled with irony. They do not rely on lyrics, but more on the image of the rock lifestyle. They do not try to illustrate; rather, they explore the mythology of rock and its heroes. As

Top: A sketch by John Lennon of himself and Yoko Ono in Amsterdam. Above: Lennon and son with his Romany Roller.

craft and politicians and fused with the music to create an expanded mixed-media experience; these ideas culminated in their most ambitious project to date, their first live performance of *The Wall* in 1980.

Other big bands like the Who have worked with laser artists, who have exhibited their work at London's Royal Academy, while power chords have combined with fire-and-brimstone spectacle in Iron Maiden's stage show. Along the same lines, but on a more static level, the gigantic stadium sets of the Rolling Stones' tours of Europe and America, with their abstract colour elements, images of cars, guitars and saxophones, and huge balloon structures succeed in fusing art and music into a total event.

Cadillac nightmares

Such spectacles grew out of the energetic artistic concerns of the Sixties, where experiment was rife and the traditional barriers between the arts were constantly under attack. It was natural for the young artist wishing to include sound elements in his work to turn to rock. The stigma of triviality so often associated with pop music by the art establishment did not concern the new breed of artists, who saw no future in the life-drawing classes of the art colleges but looked more to the immediacy of what was going on around them in the clubs, streets and pinball arcades as a source of imagery.

It remains an irony of the Sixties that while such artistic experiment was being taken out of the gallery and was reaching a far broader audience than ever before, it was destined – by its very nature – to be lost beyond the few photographs, films and

such, this book was a one-off. It has been followed by a number of greatly inferior books of rock illustration which go no further than to throw up the most superficial aspects of rock, or make very obvious and crass visual jokes with the mindless swish of the ever-present airbrush.

Pictures of Jimi

Outside the more ephemeral productions of Sixties mixed-media and the later rock illustrators lies David Oxtoby. Since the late Fifties, Oxtoby has devoted his total and extremely prolific output to the subject of rock. While a student at London's Royal Academy, Oxtoby developed a passion for rock that dominated both his work and his life; he very soon realised that these two areas were inseparable. Night after night was spent in clubs like the Flamingo in Wardour Street and later, the Bag o' Nails, in the company of musicians such as the then-unknown Jimi Hendrix. Hard drinking and wild living led Oxtoby to the black clubs of New York in the mid Sixties, the only white man in the place. And as he absorbed the music, so he put it down on canvas.

His interests are not with the musicians themselves and his pictures are not por-

Right: Guy Peellaert's mournful portrait of Hank Williams from the book Rock Dreams. *Below: Iron Maiden's apocalyptic stage show.*

traits in the conventional sense. In each work, whether it be of Gene Vincent, Elvis, Otis Redding or the Who, he aims to capture the *sound*. To this end he works while listening to his subjects' recordings, and often bases a picture on one particular song. A giant portrait of Springsteen entitled *He's The One* was inspired by the song 'She's The One', a track from the album *Born To Run* (1975). *King Lee Spring* – a large multiple portrait of Jerry Lee Lewis – is based on the song 'I Can't Stop Loving You'. This latter is particularly effective in the way different elements of the song are picked up in the painting; the razzle of the piano in the brightly coloured streamers, the tension in the powerhouse vocals translated into visual terms across the surface of the canvas.

Oxtoby has painted everyone from Bill Haley to Janis Joplin, the Big Bopper to Diana Ross. Each picture has a style of its own unique to the music from which it is drawn. Oxtoby works from photographs; earlier in his career he was concerned that meeting the objects of his portraits might muddy the process of abstracting the aural aspects of the music and putting them together with the visual elements. As each musician has a style and sound unique to themselves, so Oxtoby's pictures reflect these styles. The sweaty blacks and blues of the Otis Redding pictures, the paint applied crudely and expressionistically, stand in strong contract to the carefully-worked line and colour of a Dylan picture, *Knocking On Heaven's Door*. The contrast between the two is as strong as the contrast between the raunchy brass backing of the soul artist and Dylan's mournful death song of the sheriff from the soundtrack of the film *Pat Garrett And Billy The Kid* (1973). In a series of pictures of country artists, ranging from Johnny Cash to Hank Wangford, Oxtoby has chosen a bland, flat colour background on which the musicians' faces are drawn with minute care and attention to detail. In contrast, *Back Track* depicts Hendrix with strokes of muted colour, almost abstract save for the neck of his Stratocaster and the pristine clarity of the microphone stand.

While Oxtoby's 'Rockers' do not demand a lot of theory to be appreciated, Warhol's Elvis and Blake's rock references are part of a much wider artistic interest in mass-media imagery and in retrospect are both passing phases in the development of their work as a whole. Putting rock into art has always been the key concern in Oxtoby's work, however, and while it is useful at times to be aware of the occasional external references in his pictures, it is more important to like the music he paints about. JONATHAN REED

Two of David Oxtoby's remarkable paintings. Knocking On Heaven's Door *(top right) draws inspiration from Dylan's* Pat Garrett And Billy The Kid *soundtrack, while* Just Jimi *(right) captures Hendrix's 'controlled freedom'.*

In the Pink

The ascent of Pink Floyd from the underground to world acclaim

WRITING IN THE *San Francisco Chronicle* in late October 1966, alternative poet Kenneth Rexroth described a party he had attended in London earlier that month. This had been the *International Times* launch party at the Roundhouse and Rexroth had not enjoyed the evening. The main group, he reported, had failed to turn up and an amateur band, presumably selected from the audience, had taken their place, playing long, improvised passages of bizarre sounds and discordant noise. In fact, the main group – Pink Floyd – *had* appeared, but Rexroth, though an aficionado of San Francisco's emerging 'underground' bands, had not been prepared for anything as experimental and *weird* as this. They just *had* to be amateurs messing around, he concluded.

Although it mirrored many aspects of the San Francisco scene, London's musical underground was in many ways more adventurous than its Californian counterpart. Jefferson Airplane had roots in folk, the Grateful Dead in jug-band music and mainstream rock'n'roll, but the influences that shaped the sound of the new bands on London's alternative club circuit were a richer, more diverse mixture. There was Soft Machine – a brew of modern jazz, tape-loops and amplified motorbikes. There was Tomorrow – naive political comment, guitar feedback pyrotechnics, lunacy and mayhem.

Above: A 1967 poster advertises forthcoming events at London's UFO club. Top: Roger Waters (left) and Syd Barrett of Pink Floyd on stage in 1967. With their revolutionary light show, the Floyd were the band of the London underground.

And there was Pink Floyd – classics, country blues, beat and R&B filtered through the highly distinctive, disturbing compositions of Syd Barrett into an acid/space-rock spectacular.

Light fantastic

The London underground scene with no Pink Floyd is as hard to imagine as Merseybeat with no Beatles or British R&B without the Rolling Stones. They were virtually the house band at UFO, the club that provided the venue for the underground's 'headquarters' during 1966-67, and the highlight of all the major 'happenings' of the time – the *IT* party, 'Psychodelphia Versus Ian Smith', the '14 Hour Technicolor Dream' *et al* – was a Floyd performance. Though primitive by modern standards, their light show was – for Britain at least – revolutionary, and the throbbing, oily patterns provided a hypnotic backdrop for the eerie themes and shifting textures of the music. In the court of the London freak, Pink Floyd – and, in particular, Syd Barrett, with his dark, staring eyes and mirror-disc-covered Telecaster – were kings.

Such was the spirit of the times, back in 1967, that the group could assail the pop charts – with 'Arnold Layne' and 'See Emily Play' – without damaging their underground status and credibility. But by 1968, new trends were emerging; pop and rock had become distinct entities and rock groups were now expected to be *serious*. Creating hit singles – releasing singles at all, in fact – was distinctly 'uncool' in the world of album-oriented progressive music.

Thus, with the benefit of hindsight, one can argue that when Pink Floyd were forced to oust the increasingly erratic and unreliable Syd Barrett from their ranks in 1968, it was a blessing in disguise for the remaining group members. For Barrett had been the band's main – almost sole – writer. And if the Floyd had continued to rely upon his mad acid creations and commercial oddities, they might have gone the way of their underground contemporaries who were, by and large, dismissed by the 'progressive' consumers of the later Sixties and early Seventies. As it was, the group was forced to revaluate its musical policy and come up with a new formula; Barrett's major gift had been for surreal lyrics and quirkily catchy melodies – talents lacking in the rest of the band. The Floyd soon realised that their future lay not in attempting to build upon their previous pop success but in delving further into, and developing, the space-rock form that Barrett had virtually invented with 'Astronomy Domine'.

After Syd Barrett's departure from Pink Floyd in 1968, the group moved away from quirky melodies towards extended themes and sound exploration which required them to use a mass of equipment (below).

Pigs and octopuses

Pink Floyd's move towards long, evocative extemporisation was signalled by the release of *Ummagumma* in 1969 and set the seal on their future development. The Seventies were to see the release of a sequence of albums built around extended themes, improvisation and the exploration of sound; stage shows became increasingly more elaborate, evolving into a devastating barrage of effects including inflatable pigs, giant octopuses and flaming gongs. By the time the massive-selling *Dark Side Of The Moon* came out in 1973, Pink Floyd had become an institution – and one that remained intact a decade later via such landmarks as *Wish You Were Here* and *The Wall*.

Throughout their career, the group have maintained a low public profile, rarely granting interviews, never exciting gossip. On stage, from *Atom Heart Mother* to *The Wall*, they have remained aloof, content to allow spectacular visual tricks and myriad sound textures to take the starring roles. And rather than alienating their audience, Pink Floyd's public facelessness has merely enhanced their reputation by providing an element of mystery that has been a key factor in their continuing survival.

TOM HIBBERT

GOING UNDERGROUND

The London club scene took off with UFO

THE STORY OF THE CLUBS and musical events associated with the underground scene in London is, in many ways, the evolution of the underground itself – the two are inextricably bound up with each other. By common agreement, the first public manifestation of the phenomenon was the International Poetry Festival at the Albert Hall in June 1965, which brought together poets from the English alternative arts scene, like Pete Brown, and Americans such as Allen Ginsberg. The audience that day was full of strangely clad figures, bedecked with flowers and carrying joss-sticks – hippies were making their first public appearance in the UK.

Hazy Sunday afternoons

A number of the Americans who helped organise the event remained in London and became prime movers on the scene. One was Steve Stollman, brother of the owner of the avant-garde ESP label in New York. In February 1966 he organised the first of a series of events known as 'Spontaneous Underground', which were held at the Marquee Club on Sunday afternoons. In retrospect these events seem oddly parochial, decidedly naive and having more in common with early Sixties beatnik happenings than anything else; they were, nonetheless, the first link in the chain that led to the UFO club and beyond. The early ones featured people like Cream lyricist Pete Brown performing conjuring tricks, and strange avant-garde orchestras that utilised transistor radios, not to mention a girl playing a Bach fugue accompanied by African drummers. Then in March, Spontaneous Underground was enlivened by the appearance of an unknown band dubbed the Pink Floyd Sound. They were loud, weird and unique – and they fitted perfectly.

Over the weeks at the Marquee things developed, plans were hatched and the

Below far left: John 'Hoppy' Hopkins, co-founder of IT *and UFO. Bottom far left: Pedestrian art at the* IT *launch party, 1966. Bottom centre: Soft Machine play at the same event. Below: Pink Floyd at Middle Earth. Bottom: A hippie at Alexandra Palace, 1967.*

forces in the underground – John Hopkins, Miles (who ran Indica Books), Andrew King and Pete Jenner (who became the Floyd's managers) and Joe Boyd – all came together. The scene shifted from the Marquee to the London Free School in Notting Hill Gate, a community self-help establishment run primarily by 'Hoppy' (as Hopkins was universally known). One of its early classes was the Sound/Light Workshop, at which Pink Floyd often provided music. The group soon became the centre of interest, and All Saints Hall in Powis Square was swamped every week. The stage was set for something new and exciting involving all the various components: lights, films, dance and music.

The first big event of this 'new' underground was a party to launch *International Times* (England's first underground paper and the brainchild of Miles and Hoppy), held at the Roundhouse in Chalk Farm on 15 October 1966. Originally an engine shed, the Roundhouse had been taken over by the Gilbey's Gin concern, which had installed a balcony that stood on wooden pillars. The building had a marvellous, almost romantic atmosphere – it was a monument to nineteenth-century industrial design. Unfortunately it was cold, had almost no lighting, just two lavatories and the only entrance was via an ancient, steep and extremely narrow staircase.

Nonetheless the *IT* party was a memorable event. Some 2000 people turned up and were greeted by Miles handing out sugar-cubes (which turned out not to be of the LSD-coated variety, despite legend to the contrary). What took place set the style for later events – people in bizarre fancy dress rolling in huge bellies, dancing, revelling, tripping and watching films; a Bacchanal of the first order. Paul McCartney showed up dressed as an Arab, the Italian film director Michelangelo Antonioni was there taking a break from shooting *Blow Up* and Marianne Faithfull, wearing a nun's habit, won the prize for the 'shortest/barest' costume. Music was provided not only by Pink Floyd but also Soft Machine, whose instrumentation included a motorcycle with a contact mike attached to the cylinder head – the bike was revved up from time to time to add to the group's euphonious wailing.

Pink Floyd, meanwhile, brought with them the light show they had been using at the Free School – oil dropped on photographic slides pulsated in time with music. Within months that light show was to seem incredibly primitive, but few people had seen one before and the Roundhouse audience was transfixed. Musically the Floyd played one of their best sets, even though the power short-circuited in the middle of 'Interstellar Overdrive'.

Underground freak out

The *IT* party was also the first underground event to garner national press coverage; *The Sunday Times* ran a story on it, including an interview with Pink Floyd's Roger Waters. Over the next few months, further one-off events along the lines of the party took place. Some, like 'Psychodelphia Versus Ian Smith', were held at the Roundhouse; others, like the even more bizarrely-named 'Freak Out Ethel', were held elsewhere. However, none of them quite captured the magic of the *IT* party, especially as many (the 'New Years Eve All Night Rave' at the Roundhouse, for example) were obviously commercially-motivated ventures. But by the end of the year, the underground had found a new centre – at UFO, the Friday night club founded by Hoppy (aided and abetted by Joe Boyd and Miles) that had grown out of the Free School.

Below: An audience sits and 'grooves' to the sounds and lights at UFO. Until its demise in October 1967, the club served as headquarters of the London underground scene. Inset: Granny Takes A Trip, a popular hippie clothes outlet.

UFO was located in an Irish dance-hall called the Blarney Club in the basement of 31 Tottenham Court Road, opposite the Dominion Theatre, and opened on 23 December 1966. At first, the club was titled 'UFO Presents Night Tripper'; the 'Night' part was relevant as UFO always hosted all-night events, a factor that put it out of the reach of many hippies, especially young ones and those with day-jobs.

The UFO legend has grown over the years and, as Roger Waters has said, 'It's got rosier with age, but there is a germ of truth in it.' So what actually happened there? It certainly wasn't just a club in the entertainment sense; it was a genuine meeting/market place for the underground. For the first couple of months virtually everyone knew everyone else who was packed inside and sniffed the overpowering aroma of sweat and dope. Deals were made and projects planned. One could buy hippie paraphernalia from the 'head' shop or a frilly shirt from John Pearce's Granny Takes A Trip stall. Later on, more intense activities took place in backrooms, like black activist Michael X relieving liberals of 'conscience' money for one of his schemes or Michael Henshaw (accountant to the underground and the 'responsible' face of UFO) trying to arrange bail for someone. It was a remarkably relaxed environment, in which the likes of Mick Jagger or John Lennon could sit all night without being pestered for autographs.

And then there was the entertainment itself, with which UFO refined the previous mixed-media attempts into a heady brew that has never been equalled. Some

Above left: Poster for the 14 Hour Technicolor Dream. With 41 groups on the bill and over 10,000 people in the audience (above), this turned out to be the London underground's biggest event.

nights it did bear more relation to the early Sixties – tired poets reading their works to the backing of jazz combos – but generally, especially when Pink Floyd played, it was magic. When UFO started Hoppy had given the Floyd the contract to provide music and lights at the club. Although the group didn't play at UFO every week, it's fair to say that the club was home base for the band and it always gave them a chance to play for an audience that understood and loved their music.

Helter-skelter
UFO also attracted many of the new bands who were springing up in the wake of the Floyd. Some went on to some degree of fame and fortune, notably Soft Machine, perhaps the most intellectual of them all. Others included Arthur Brown (he of the flaming head-dress), the Purple Gang (who recorded 'Granny Takes A Trip', a UFO anthem), Tomorrow (featuring singer Keith West, future Yes guitarist Steve Howe and a great line in theatrics) and Procul Harum, who played at UFO the week their 'A Whiter Shade Of Pale' went to Number 1.

Not everyone thought that UFO – or the underground in general – was wonderful, however. There was increasingly abusive coverage in the press, and at the beginning of April 1967 the police raided the offices of *IT* in a calculated attempt to close the

paper down. In order to raise money a benefit event was put together. 'The 14 Hour Technicolor Dream', as it was called, took place at Alexandra Palace on 29 April and it turned out to be the biggest single underground event – though it is a curious paradox that something that attracted over 10,000 people could be described as 'underground'. This immense crowd turned up to watch the 41 bands, listen to poetry, see films and ride the helter-skelter. There were two stages with bands playing simultaneously, which with the various light shows was almost too much to take in. Soft Machine were in top form – Kevin Ayers in cowboy hat surmounted by aeroplane wings, Daevid Allen in miner's helmet – but once again it was Pink Floyd who stole the show, coming on as the first light of dawn poured through the high windows, their eerie sounds echoing around the building. In retrospect, the Technicolor Dream was not only the biggest and best underground event but also the last genuine one.

Back at UFO things were starting to go awry; basically it was too small to accommodate the increasing number of visitors. The original 'freaks' and hippies had been largely displaced by unwelcome newcomers; at best, these were 'weekend hippies', at worst they were drunken sailors (who took the idea of 'free love' a little too literally) or hippie-bashing skinheads.

The crunch came in June, when Hoppy was imprisoned for drug offences. Police pressure on the club increased in the following weeks, resulting in the landlords revoking the lease. The club moved into the Roundhouse but, despite the fact that the building was still almost derelict, the rent was exorbitant. When a big name like Eric Burdon or Jeff Beck was playing, UFO broke even, but the club more often lost money. The Roundhouse may have been a good place for special events, but the atmosphere of the club evaporated in the cold emptiness of the building. UFO stuck it out until October and then folded – for many people it was the end of an era.

Part-time hippies

That summer of 1967 had represented the height, in public terms, of the new alternative culture; by the autumn it had sunk, very nearly without trace. From being the property of a committed minority the previous winter, it had spread with remarkable speed throughout the country, falling prey to over-commercialisation; neck-bells tinkled in high streets across the country and by September flower power had become a national joke. The music suffered too. Any band that had been remotely kaftan-and-bell-oriented was in danger of being laughed off stage.

Pockets of resistance held out, however, and a few clubs continued something approximating to a UFO style. UFO had not been the only club with an underground atmosphere and clientele at the time, but the others were without exception more overtly commercial enterprises. One of the best was Happening 44, located at 44 Gerrard Street in Soho and run by Jack Bracelin, who had been part of the Free School Light/Sound workshop where he had developed his own light show. The Social Deviants (with Mick Farren) was virtually Happening 44's houseband.

Better-known than Happening 44, however, was Middle Earth in Covent Garden. This had evolved from the Electric Garden

Above: Dancing and hanging around at the Roundhouse, 1967. Below: Spandau Ballet's Martin Kemp (right) with Steve Strange, whose occasional clubs in the Eighties resurrected the ideals of UFO.

which had opened a few months after UFO but, despite interesting bills, had never taken off. Yoko Ono was supposed to have sensed 'bad vibrations' on the opening night – possibly because the club was run by two East End gangsters. After a couple of months it closed and then reopened as Middle Earth. It was still run on commercial lines but the new owners wisely employed hippies as organisers of the club, notably Dave Howson, who had been one of the organisers of the 'Technicolor Dream'. While UFO was still in operation, Middle Earth diplomatically closed on Friday nights.

After the demise of UFO, however, Middle Earth took over as the main under-

ground music club. The club's policy was, in some ways, less adventurous than that of UFO, but their more commercial nature meant they were able to book a lot of big-name artists, especially from the United States; over the following year Tim Buckley, Captain Beefheart, the Byrds and even the Ike and Tina Turner Revue played in Covent Garden. Also, like UFO, Middle Earth tried out the Roundhouse for a few gigs, including the major coup of putting on Jefferson Airplane and the Doors in September 1968. Shortly after, however, the club folded, another victim of dwindling finances and police pressure. Arguably, Middle Earth was the last genuine underground club, although mention should be made of the Temple, which in 1969 operated out of the basement of the old Flamingo Club in Wardour Street. The Temple was probably the seediest rock venue London has ever had and attracted a clientele to match its sordid decor: acid casualties, speed freaks, shysters and thieves.

By 1969, the underground – superficially, at least – had more adherents than ever before; in reality, however, it simply meant there were more people (particularly in the suburbs) with long hair who took LSD. Any connection they may have had with the early UFO crowd was accidental and their meeting places – the Midnight Court at the Lyceum (run by Mecca) and Implosion at the Roundhouse – lie outside this history.

The underground clubs and events were, of course, a product of their time and thus can never be duplicated. However, the clubs and events arranged by Steve Strange in the early Eighties, with their emphasis on performance art and esoteric atmosphere, resurrected some of the ideas, if not the spirit, of UFO.   JOHN PLATT

WELCOME TO THE MACHINE

How Pink Floyd set the controls for success

PINK FLOYD was formed by Roger Keith (Syd) Barrett, George Roger Waters, Richard William Wright and Nicholas Berkeley Mason in London during the latter part of 1965. Syd Barrett and Roger Waters both attended Cambridge High School for Boys, where Dave Gilmour, who would subsequently replace Barrett on guitar in the group, had been a fellow pupil. On leaving Cambridge, Barrett enrolled at Camberwell School of Art in London, the classic type of establishment for any aspiring Sixties pop star. There he applied a certain amount of paint to canvas, but became increasingly interested in playing the guitar. Gilmour was also in London at the time and ironically taught Barrett many of his early chords.

Waters also left Cambridge for London, but he opted for the rather more prosaic environs of the Regent Street Polytechnic and a course in architecture. There he met Nick Mason and Rick Wright on the same course and the three quickly discovered a mutual interest in forming a group, the first version of which was called Sigma 6 and had no success in securing a recording contract. At this point, Wright could already play piano, harmonium, harpsichord and cello, while Mason, an accomplished tympanist, was of more immediate practical use in providing the money for the group's early equipment.

Other names and line-ups followed, including the T-Set, the Abdabs and the Screaming Abdabs and all met with the same fate. Eventually, Waters on bass, Mason on drums and Wright on keyboards made one final attempt to make it work, bringing in two new members, a jazz guitarist called Bob Close and Syd Barrett, who was still friendly with Waters from Cambridge days. Barrett, in a typical burst of lateral thinking, named the group the Pink Floyd Sound after a pair of old bluesmen called Pink Anderson and Floyd Council. Barrett and Close did not get on

Right: At the gates of fame – the psychedelic Pink Floyd in 1967. Clockwise from top left: Nick Mason, Rick Wright, Syd Barrett and Roger Waters.

Given the experimental sights and sounds of Pink Floyd's new stage act, they were a natural choice as the resident group.

The next step was to release a single to capitalise on the band's popularity. This duly appeared at the beginning of 1967, produced by UFO co-founder Joe Boyd. Released on EMI's Columbia label, to whom the group had signed for a reputed £5000 advance, the single was called 'Arnold Layne'. It was written by Barrett and, far from being some vague experiment in feedback, it turned out to be a pithy ditty concerning the activities of a young man who steals ladies' underwear from washing lines, and it was promptly banned by a number of radio stations. This affected sales to an extent, but the single still reached Number 20 in the charts.

Meanwhile the group were using numerous live dates as a testing ground for an increasingly ambitious range of material. Dates varied from small clubs to another *IT* extravaganza at London's Alexandra Palace, 'The 14 Hour Technicolor Dream Free Speech Festival', and most ambitiously a solo concert at the Queen Elizabeth Hall. The event was entitled 'Games For May', and it saw the group make their first tentative step to improving the dire standards of sound prevalent at the time by installing speakers at the back of the hall to give a primitive version of quadrophonic sound. As well as being the title of the event, 'Games For May' was also a new Syd Barrett song and with a change of name and lyrics it became their second single.

At the gates

On 22 June 1967, 'See Emily Play' hit the charts and spent 12 weeks there, peaking at Number 6. Although again on Columbia, the group had undergone a change of producer, Joe Boyd having been replaced by staff man Norman Smith at EMI's insistence. The fact that Pink Floyd did not have another hit single for 12 years after this gives an indication of the change of direction that was already imminent. On 5 August of that year, Pink Floyd released their debut LP, *The Piper At The Gates Of Dawn*; the title had been culled by Barrett from one of the most popular underground reading manuals, Kenneth Grahame's *The Wind In The Willows*.

The material on the LP reflected Syd Barrett's dominance of the group at this stage in its development; of the 11 tracks on the record Barrett had wholly or co-written 10 – the only exception was a minor effort from Waters called 'Take Up Thy Stethoscope And Walk'. Not content with this, Barrett also provided the artwork for the back of the cover. The first track on the first side spelled out the direction in which Pink Floyd were heading and was in marked contrast to the group's first two singles; 'Astronomy Domine' was a dynamic space anthem that was to remain one of the highlights of the Floyd's repertoire for years to come. On 24 October 1967 Pink Floyd began their first tour of the US,

together and shortly afterwards Close left the group as a result of one of the earliest recorded examples of 'musical differences'.

Games on the underground

The four-piece line-up now secured their first regular dates on Sunday afternoons at the Marquee Club in London's Wardour Street during a series of concerts with the generic title of 'Spontaneous Underground', which commenced in February 1966. The group's set at this time was a weird mixture of straight R&B tunes such as 'Roadrunner' and interludes of imaginative instrument abuse as the group explored the possibilities of feedback. Later that year the group discovered the other element that was to transform their stage shows and make them the house band of underground London. During a series of dates at the London Free School's Sound/Light Workshop, held in All Saint's Church Hall in Notting Hill Gate, Pink Floyd met an American couple called Joel

and Toni Brown, both of whom were students of Timothy Leary. Together they conceived the idea of using a rudimentary lightshow during the performance with brightly coloured slides projected on the group.

On 15 October 1966, Pink Floyd consummated its affair with the underground by playing at the launch party for *International Times*, the first newspaper to be produced specifically for the alternative culture. The Floyd played to an audience of over 2000 and the response confirmed that the group had found an identity and a following which was to be the stepping stone to future success. At the end of that same month, the four members of the group together with then-manager Peter Jenner and Andrew King formed Blackhill Enterprises as a partnership to run the group's business affairs. The upswing in their fortunes was confirmed on 23 December 1966 when the legendary UFO club first opened its doors in Tottenham Court Road.

On stage, the Floyd members have always played second fiddle to spectacular effects. Opposite: The band play before film of prime minister Edward Heath, 1972. Above: Amid smoke the same year.

taking British psychedelia to an amazed and then appreciative audience in the country where it had all started. The focal point was inevitably Barrett, whose deranged stage presence was pushed to manic extremes by his constant intake of large amounts of LSD. Barrett's erratic behaviour was making it increasingly difficult for his fellow group members to work with him, and his days with the Floyd were numbered.

Another symptom of the growing malaise was the delay in releasing the group's third single. Another Barrett composition, entitled 'Apples And Oranges', it took an inordinately long time to record and, following its eventual release on 18 November 1967, flopped disastrously. The failure of the single, together with Barrett's general state of mind, made a change of musical policy inevitable. It duly arrived in the shape of Dave Gilmour who, since teaching Barrett the rudiments of the guitar, had pursued a nomadic existence in Europe with his own group. He spent some time in Paris where he learned French and also worked for a time as a male model. Gilmour joined the group in February as second guitarist, although it was widely realised what the eventual outcome would be. Barrett's mental state made it impossible for him to carry on and a matter of weeks after Gilmour's arrival Syd was asked to leave the group.

During the Barrett period, Pink Floyd had been a distinctly schizophrenic outfit, with a devoted but relatively small underground following for their live performances and their more ambitious musical output. They also enjoyed a more general appreciation among young pop fans for their quirky singles and appearances on BBC-TV's 'Top Of The Pops'. The group deliberately turned its back on the latter (potentially more lucrative) market and devoted its energies solely to LPs, a policy it resolutely maintained thereafter.

Pink Floyd continued to enhance their live reputation by playing a wide range of dates. The equally legendary Middle Earth club had superseded UFO, and the band played this venue several times to general acclaim. Although Blackhill Enterprises had became divorced from Pink Floyd's management during the upheaval of Barrett's departure (he remained with Blackhill), the company was busily engaged in promoting the first of what would become traditional London events: the Hyde Park free concerts. On 29 June 1968 Pink Floyd headlined the first free concert in the park on a bill that included Jethro Tull and Roy

Harper. June was a significant month for the group in that it also marked the release of their second album, A Saucerful Of Secrets. Playing without the charismatic Barrett on stage in front of a large audience and producing an LP without his songwriting abilities represented a doubly searching test of the new formation's strengths, and the confidence they gained by passing both ordeals bolstered the group immeasurably. In fact the LP did contain one Barrett composition, 'Jugband Blues', but it was, to all intents and purposes, a triumph for the new line-up – and in particular Waters, whose 'Set The Controls For The Heart Of The Sun' became another live favourite, with its simple repeated phrase providing the launching pad for sundry instrumental pyrotechnics.

Azimuth and Auximenes

Another extensive bout of touring followed, with visits to all parts of Europe and then a further assault on the American concert circuit later in 1968. The group spent a lot of time and money in developing a sound system that could accurately reproduce their increasingly sophisticated musical effects. The results of this research were formally unveiled in London's Festival Hall on 14 April 1969 in the shape of the Azimuth Co-ordinator. The event was entitled, with a suitable flourish, 'More Furious Madness From The Massed

Gadgets Of Auximenes'. The Azimuth device was basically a rotating control stick, and while the basic drum and bass sound thundered out of the main PA system, the control stick was used to send a barrage of electronic effects whirling from speaker to speaker around the audience.

With this concert and the subsequent tour with a show called more simply 'The Journey', Pink Floyd broke out of the restricting confines of being a psychedelic band and reached a larger audience. With the exception of Syd Barrett, the group had never espoused the philosophy of LSD. The group was later quoted as saying: 'Our attitude to freak-outs is that we would not play at one again unless they paid us three times our normal fee.' Roger Waters was even more scathing: 'There was so much dope and acid around in those days that I don't think anyone can remember anything about anything.'

Cymbaline in the cinema
Given the extended atmospheric pieces for which Pink Floyd were becoming renowned, it was a logical diversification for the group to get involved in producing film music – so when Barbet Schroeder offered them a considerable sum to write the music for a film he was directing called *More*, they were happy to accept. And it was a number entitled 'Cymbaline', from the soundtrack LP released in 1969, that first gained a radio breakthrough for the group in the United States and brought them to the attention of a wider audience.

It was the group's next album that established them as a major force in 'progressive' music. Released in October 1969 on EMI's newly-formed underground label, Harvest, *Ummagumma* was a double LP,

Inset top: Roger Waters. Above: Nick Mason. Below: The Floyd take France by storm, 1974.

half of which had been recorded live earlier that year on dates in Manchester and Birmingham. The live album perfectly captured the atmospheric intensity of the Floyd's electric stage performances as they ran through their space anthems, 'Astronomy Domine' and 'Set The Controls For The Heart Of The Sun', as well as 'A Saucerful Of Secrets' and the truly chilling 'Careful With That Axe, Eugene'.

The second record saw the group in an experimental vein, with each band member given an equal amount of room for compositions; although such contributions as Wright's 'Sysyphus' or Waters' 'Several Species Of Small Furry Animals Gathered Together In A Cave And Grooving With A Pict' seem self-indulgent in retrospect, they were quite in keeping with the nature of the 'progressive' era. *Ummagumma*'s cover, meanwhile, gave some indication as to how the group – who always maintained a low public profile, the members never parading themselves as 'stars' – viewed itself. On the front were mysteriously changing mirror images of the group members, while the reverse showed their barrage of equipment laid out on the tarmac of a runway – suggesting, or so it seemed, that the electric tools of the Floyd's trade were as important as the personalities within the group itself.

During much of 1970 the group remained out of the public eye until the release in October of *Atom Heart Mother*, complete with a striking Hipgnosis cover depicting a cow. The title track was an extended piece that included choral and orchestral segments alongside guitar solos. This was balanced by a more conventional second side that contained some of the band's most relaxed work, including

Inset top: Guitarist Dave Gilmour, who took over from Syd Barrett in 1968. Above: Rick Wright at the keyboards.

the wry humour of 'Alan's Psychedelic Breakfast'; in subsequent live dates, tea was made on stage during this number. The group took the work to America at the end of the year, accompanied by a 10-piece orchestral group and a choir of 20. Together with the 360-degree sound system, the show made quite an impression on audiences. The *LA Free Press* noted in astonishment that, rather than dancing, the 'freaks' in the audience actually sat down and listened to the music, while Roger Waters commented: 'Our idea is to put the sound all around the audience with ourselves in the middle. Then the performance becomes more theatrical – it can include melodrama, literary things, music and lights.'

Obscured by the moon
15 May 1971 saw the group in action at a Crystal Palace Garden Party, complete with a giant inflatable octopus which rose from the lake in front of the stage. The set featured a new piece called 'Return To The Sun Of Nothing'; on 13 November this was to surface as 'Echoes', forming the second side of the band's new LP *Meddle*.

Although 'Echoes' was a beautifully constructed, seductive and atmospheric piece, it gave signs that the Floyd's development might be slowing down. As Nick Mason commented: 'There are similarities between *Atom Heart Mother* and *Meddle* and there are various things in the construction [of 'Echoes'] that have a Pink Floyd flavour but are also very dangerous Pink Floyd clichés. One is the possible tendency to get stuck into a sort of slow four tempo. And the other thing is to take a melody line and flog it to death.'

Much of the year was taken up by a mammoth world tour, while 1972 found the Floyd again lying low; their only activity was to release another soundtrack album, *Obscured By Clouds*, from another Barbet Schroeder film, *La Vallée*. The American public again took to Pink Floyd's film music and, although *Atom Heart Mother* had reached Number 1 in the UK, it was only with this LP that the group started to sell records in great quantities in the US.

This relatively quiet period was fully explained the following year with the release of *Dark Side Of The Moon*, which burst upon an unsuspecting rock press at a preview held in the London Planetarium in March 1973. The group was now producing itself and the result of nearly a year's painstaking efforts was an LP of startling clarity and power. The ultimate technical compliment was paid when it was revealed that hi-fi buffs were buying the record simply to test the quality of their equipment. The songs on the LP – titles included 'Brain Damage', 'Money' and 'Time' – dealt with a very dark side of life and this indicated the Floyd's growing interest in doomy themes. 'We sat in a rehearsal room and Roger came up with the specific idea of dealing with all the things that drive people mad,' Wright later said.

The subsequent tour featuring the material was suitably epic, with a soul vocal group called the Blackberries used on the US dates. By the time Pink Floyd played at London's Earl's Court in May, they had perfected a show with a dazzling array of special effects, including a flaming gong, a creature with green laser eyes and an aeroplane that swooped from the back of the hall and crashed on stage in blinding light and smoke.

Pink Floyd performing The Wall *in 1980. Right: The grotesque figure of the teacher wields his cane as the band play on regardless. Below: The group line up with Pink Floyd 'doubles'.*

The band then spent over two years attempting to produce a worthy successor to *Dark Side Of The Moon*, such were the pressures its worldwide success had created. The outcome was *Wish You Were Here*, released in September 1975, and it was rather predictably given a lukewarm reception. The LP had some fine moments, however, notably the tribute to Syd Barrett called 'Shine On You Crazy Diamond'. It was only with the release of *Animals* in February 1977 that Pink Floyd regained critical favour. As on *Dark Side Of The Moon*, Waters' songs dealt with the unacceptable facets of life, and his view of the human condition is reflected both in the song titles – 'Pigs', 'Dogs' and 'Sheep' – and in uncompromisingly bleak lyrics. The tours were given added power by the ex-

tensive use of film, projected on a circular screen behind the band, additional musicians to boost the sound and an inflatable pig which was very much the album's symbol. The cover featured one flying over Battersea power station and caused endless problems when it was photographed on a windy day.

While the other three members of the group had produced solo efforts relatively quickly – David Gilmour's eponymous album and Wright's *Wet Dream* were both released in 1978, while Mason had done production work for Principal Edwards' Magic Theatre, Unicorn, Robert Wyatt and others – Roger Waters' effort was longer in gestation. It eventually appeared as a double LP credited to the group, but was in most respects Waters' own creation.

Up against The Wall

As *The Wall*, it was released on 30 November 1979. The songs were linked by the presence of a central character called Pink who, through a series of trials and tribulations, becomes a powerful symbol of society's oppression of the individual. The single 'Another Brick In The Wall (Part Two)', taken from the LP, soared into the UK charts on 1 December 1979 and subsequently became the band's first Number 1 single despite its unlikely content – a savage indictment of the educational system. The live performances of *The Wall* were dominated by the construction of an enormous wall during the course of the set that gradually obscured the group from view. A band of Pink Floyd doubles then took the stage, while the real group played on invisibly. At the climax of the performance, the wall crashed down and the group emerged with acoustic instruments.

Wright, Gilmour, Mason and Waters all produced further solo albums, Wright as Zee with new wave guitarist Dee Harris. But only Waters, whose *Pros And Cons Of Hitch-Hiking* (1984) was promoted with a tour set including many Floyd classics, came close to enhancing his reputation.

It was no surprise, then, when Pink Floyd reformed—without Waters, who went to law in an unsuccessful atempt to stop them using the name—and recorded *A Momentary Lapse Of Reason* (1987). Despite the lack of their principal writer, the album sold well in both the US and UK; *The Final Cut*, it seemed, had been premature.

Aside from the lasting power and beauty of much of their music, one of the main achievements of Pink Floyd lies in their uncompromising search for perfection in sound and presentation. After the chaos of the psychedelic era, the group pioneered a sound of the highest quality in both their recorded and live work. Both albums and concerts have been characterised by an attention to detail that has made them monumental experiences and the group was to influence a new generation of artists of the Seventies—Yes, Mike Oldfield, Genesis *et al*—who valued musicianship and presentation above all else PETER CLARK

PINK FLOYD
Discography to 1983

Singles
Arnold Layne/Candy And A Currant Bun (Columbia DB 8156, 1967); See Emily Play/Scarecrow (Columbia DB 8214, 1967); Apples And Oranges/Paintbox (Columbia DB 8310, 1967); It Would Be So Nice/Julia Dream (Columbia DB 8410, 1968); Point Me At The Sky/Careful With That Axe, Eugene (Columbia DB 8511, 1968); Another Brick In The Wall (Part Two)/One Of My Turns (Harvest HAR 5194, 1979); When The Tigers Broke Free/Bring The Boys Back Home (Harvest HAR 5222, 1982).

Albums
The Piper At The Gates Of Dawn (Columbia SCX 6157, 1967); *A Saucerful Of Secrets* (Columbia SCX 6258, 1968); *More* (Columbia SCX 6345, 1969); *Ummagumma* (Harvest SHDW 1/2, 1969); *Atom Heart Mother* (Harvest SHVL 781, 1970); *Relics* (Starline SRS 5071, 1971); *Meddle* (Harvest SHVL 795, 1971); *Obscured By Clouds* (Harvest SHSP 4020, 1972); *The Dark Side Of The Moon* (Harvest SHVL 804, 1973); *Wish You Were Here* (Harvest SHVL 814, 1975); *Animals* (Harvest SHVL 815, 1977); *The Wall* (Harvest SHDW 411, 1979); *A Collection Of Great Dance Songs* (Harvest SHVL 822, 1981); *The Final Cut* (Harvest SHPF 1983, 1983).

PINK FLOYD DIARY

1944
6 March David Gilmour born, Cambridge.
6 September George Roger Waters born, Cambridge.

1945
27 January Nicholas Berkeley Mason born, Birmingham.
28 July Richard William Wright born, London.

1946
6 January Roger Keith (Syd) Barrett born, Cambridge.

1965
Waters, Mason and Wright, all students at Regent Street Polytechnic, form R&B band Sigma 6. Towards the end of the year, following numerous personnel and name changes, new guitarist Syd Barrett dubs the group the Pink Floyd Sound.

1966
March Pink Floyd secure their first regular dates at the Marquee Club's Sunday afternoon 'Spontaneous Underground' sessions.
15 October Having established themselves as *the* band of London's 'underground' scene, the Floyd play at the launch party for *International Times* at the Roundhouse.
31 October Band sign a management deal with Peter Jenner and Andrew King.
12 December Pink Floyd perform at the Royal Albert Hall.

1967
February The group turn professional and record their first single, 'Arnold Layne', at Sound Techniques Studios, Chelsea.
11 March 'Arnold Layne' is released on EMI's Columbia label; the record peaks at Number 20 the following month.
29 April The band gives a celebrated performance at 'The 14 Hour Technicolor Dream Free Speech Festival' at Alexandra Palace.
12 May 'Games For May' concert at the Queen Elizabeth Hall, London.
July Pink Floyd appear three times on 'Top Of The Pops', performing their second hit 'See Emily Play'.
5 August The band's debut album, *The Piper At The Gates Of Dawn*, is released.
26 October American audiences get their first glimpse of the Floyd when the band play at the Fillmore West, San Francisco.

1968
18 February Dave Gilmour officially joins the band as second guitarist to compensate for Barrett's increasingly erratic performances.
6 April Syd Barrett's departure from Pink Floyd is announced.
12 April 'It Would Be So Nice', written by Wright, is released. It flops.
29 June The week following the release of their second album, *A Saucerful Of Secrets*, the Floyd perform at the first free concert to be held in Hyde Park.
17 December A new single, 'Point Me At The Sky', written by Waters, is released. It is another flop.

1969
14 April The band unveil their Azimuth Co-ordinator at London's Festival Hall in an event titled 'More Furious Madness From The Massed Gadgets Of Auximenes'.
July The soundtrack from the film *More*, written and performed by Pink Floyd, is released.
October *Ummagumma*, a double set comprised of one live LP (recorded at Birmingham's Mother's Club and Manchester College of Commerce) and one cut in the studio, is released on EMI's new 'progressive' label Harvest.

1970
January *The Madcap Laughs*, Syd Barrett's solo debut, on which he is backed by members of Soft Machine, issued in UK.
10 October *Atom Heart Mother* released.
November Syd Barrett's second LP, *Barrett*, is released.

1971
Throughout the year, the Floyd undertake extensive tours of Britain, Europe, Japan, Australia and America, while November sees the release of a new album, *Meddle*.

1972
17 February The group play the first of four sell-out dates at London's Rainbow Theatre. A bootleg album, *Pink Floyd Live*, is recorded at the show and, despite its illegality, sells an estimated 120,000 copies.
3 June *Obscured By Clouds* is issued. It consists of music written for *La Vallée*, a film directed by Barbet Schroeder, who was also responsible for *More*.
September The film *Pink Floyd Live At Pompeii*, directed by Adrian Maben, is premiered.

1973
March *Dark Side Of The Moon* is released; the album tops the charts on both sides of the Atlantic, remaining in the British best-seller lists for 180 weeks and the American rankings for 132.

1974
4 November Pink Floyd kick off another UK tour at the Usher Hall, Edinburgh.

1975
5 July Pink Floyd are the highlight of the Knebworth Festival.
15 September *Wish You Were Here* is released. Like its predecessor, it is a massive global success.

1976
3 December An enormous inflatable pink pig, filled with helium gas, is flown over London's Battersea power station to be photographed for the cover of *Animals*.

1977
21 January *Animals* is released.
April The band embark on a 26-date two-month tour of America.

1978
25 May David Gilmour's eponymous solo album is released.
November Richard Wright releases a solo LP, *Wet Dream*.

1979
16 November 'Another Brick In The Wall Part Two', the first Pink Floyd single for 11 years, is released. Within a week it is at Number 1 in the UK, having sold over 300,000 copies.
30 November Ambitious double set, *The Wall*, is issued. Production of the album cost over £300,000, but the investment is soon recouped – by the end of the following January it has grossed over £10 million.

1980
7 February First live performance of *The Wall* at Los Angeles Sports Arena.
4 August The first of six performances of *The Wall* at Earl's Court, London.

1982
July *The Wall*, a film directed by Alan Parker, written by Waters and featuring Boomtown Rat Bob Geldof in the starring role, opens in London to mixed reviews.

1983
March Release of *The Final Cut* LP coincides with the departure of Richard Wright to pursue various solo projects.

1984
March Gilmour releases second solo LP, *About Face*.
May Waters tours to promote *The Pros And Cons Of Hitch-Hiking* with all-star band including Eric Clapton.

1985
July Nick Mason and 10CC guitarist Rick Fenn release *Profiles;* it fails to sell.

1987
June Waters releases his second solo LP, *Radio KAOS*.
September Gilmour and Mason, who have reformed group with Wright as free-lance player, release *A Momentary Lapse Of Reason*. Reaches Number 3 in UK.

1988
October Release of Syd Barrett LP *Opel*, containing out-takes from his first two albums. Despite much media interest and an album of cover versions from independent label bands, *Beyond The Wildwood*, he remains a recluse.

NEVILLE WIGGINS

CELLULOID FLOYD

Soundtracks cement the path to The Wall

AFTER THE GERMAN experimental groups Can and Popul Vuh, both of whom gained a name early in their careers for cinema soundtrack work, Pink Floyd have – in Europe at least – done the most to marry rock music with the cinema. All three bands came from a similar, artistic, avant-garde background. Can worked with Jerzy Skolimowsky on *Deep End,* contributed to *Mädchen mit Gewalt* and scored Wim Wenders' *Alice In The Cities;* Popul

Vuh became synonymous with the director Werner Herzog, scoring many of his films including 1982's *Fitzcarraldo;* and the Floyd worked briefly with the director Barbet Schroeder, produced their own *Live At Pompeii* and eventually gained cinematic notoriety with 1982's mammoth *The Wall.*

Born in Teheran, Schroeder had joined the Beat-hippie nomads, roaming through Europe and America. Arriving in Paris in the early Sixties, he worked as a writer, jazz promoter and critic before getting the important break of assisting Jean-Luc Godard in the filming of *Les Caribiniers* in

1963. After a number of minor, self-produced and directed films, Schroeder set about the production of *More* in 1968. A story of love and drug addiction set in and around Paris, the film was begun before the 1968 riots, but inevitably became tinged by the atmosphere of the times. Finally released in 1969, the film and accompanying soundtrack album were hailed by the so-called 'head' community.

Valleys and volcanoes
Not surprisingly, the Floyd's contributions to *More,* by necessity subordinated to the film which they accompanied, were far closer to the preceding LP, *A Saucerful Of Secrets,* than to 1969's pivotal double album *Ummagumma.* A year later, prior to the lavish production of *Atom Heart Mother,* they made a similarly piecemeal contribution to Michelangelo Antonioni's *Zabriskie Point,* a film that looked terrific at

Above left: Bob Geldof as Pink in The Wall.
Above: The soundtrack album More, *released in 1969.*

that time, but, in retrospect, appears little more than a gaudy personal indulgence steeped in Sixties liberalism.

Barbet Schroeder, meanwhile, had been travelling around the South Pacific filming a documentary among the people of Papua New Guinea. He eventually brought these alarmingly-masked, but quite peaceful natives together with a group of rich Anglo-French hippies seeking the 'truth', and added the Floyd's music. On its release in 1972, *La Vallée* was described by *Time Out* magazine as a 'Journey to the Centre of a Cliché'.

But *La Vallée* was sumptuously photographed by Nestor Almendros, and the soundtrack displayed some of the most elegiac, romantic music the group had written in years, shortcircuiting the growing formalism of their post-*Meddle* studio work to return to the haunting sounds of *Ummagumma.* But Schroeder was hardly a Herzog, nor the Floyd a screen composing unit with the gift of Herzog collaborator Florian Fricke, and it is the tropical setting that carries the film. The two sides diverged sharply afterwards, the Floyd winning mass acceptance while Schroeder disappeared back into the French film industry, resurfacing in 1976 with the controversial *Maîtresse*.

Pink Floyd's next movie, *Live At Pompeii*, directed by the West German Adrian Maben, was released in 1973. Based on a performance in a Roman auditorium at Pompeii, to which no audience had been invited, it tipped the balance the other way, subordinating the visuals to the music. It best captures the dream/trance quality of their earlier pieces of music – 'A Saucerful Of Secrets', 'Careful With That Axe, Eugene' and the like – by mixing footage of the band live with a 'treated' and screened camera roaming the ruins, occasionally returning to interview a band member.

Comfortably numb?

The Wall, the Floyd's next film, quickly became the subject of intense controversy. Like *Live At Pompeii* and unlike their earlier cinematic efforts, the visuals were intended to illustrate Pink Floyd's existing music and lyrics; this was the film of the stage show of the concept album. *Dark Side Of The Moon* had rocketed the group to the top of the charts, casting off their 'underground' past and glueing them to the nation's coffee tables. The demands of their touring and recording schedules, along with the complexity and ambitiousness of their projects, were distancing them from their public and, in many ways, from financial, creative and logistic reality. Although the Floyd carried an enormous audience with them, by the time their massive stage performance of *The Wall* appeared before tens of thousands at Earls

Above: Pink Floyd are filmed in a deserted Roman amphitheatre for Live At Pompeii, *released in 1973. Bottom: In a surrealistic scene from* The Wall, *the neurotic rock star Pink tunes in.*

Court in 1980, recession and the rise of punk made them seem all the more like antiquated dinosaurs.

Roger Waters' tale of an increasingly neurotic rock star rehearsing his paranoias and delusions of grandeur in his wrecked hotel room not only reflected this situation, but was defined by it. Problems with the original staging forced the group to reoccupy the massive Earls Court stadium to enable director Alan Parker to re-shoot the live footage of the wall being built. If the original performance – involving flying pig and crashing airplane gimmicks, plus the tailor-made wall, doubles for the individual members, the army of roadies building the wall and the inflated Gerald Scarfe models – seemed almost grotesque in its theatrical excess, the cinema version was, if anything, more so. The tabloids loudly cheered the premiere of *The Wall* but less populist publications criticised the misogyny, misanthropy and underlying fascism of the film. The first live performances of *The Wall* had sparked similar fears in many.

Despite individual opinions of the music on the double album of *The Wall*, it is the quite crucial balance between Waters, the protagonist Pink and Bob Geldof who plays him, along with factors such as animator Gerald Scarfe, Alan Parker and the widely-reported bickering between all of those involved, that informs the whole tone of the film. Like his fellow cartoonist Ralph Steadman, Scarfe often treads a fine line of irony. At Waters' behest he chose, along with Waters himself and director Parker, to walk a most dangerous ironical path, for the final result is most dissatisfying in moral terms. Waters set out to do more than merely surpass The Who's *Tommy* in terms of rock spectacle, and in doing so caused much controversy.

Where other groups such as the Cure, the Residents or Throbbing Gristle have tried to use film to enhance their music, Pink Floyd have responded passively to the medium with the exception of *The Wall*. Their cinematic peak, if one can be found, was with *La Vallée*. It may be dismissed as a more exotic version of that era's obsession with the Katmandu Trail, but it did see both group and director looking for a new, different mixture of sound and vision. Had they continued on this more adventurous course, they could have paralleled Fricke and Herzog; sadly, what followed was pure suburbia.   JOHN GILL

CRAZY DIAMOND

Syd Barrett: the tragedy of Floyd's founding genius

EARLY IN 1970, *Melody Maker* asked Roger Waters what he thought of *The Madcap Laughs*, the debut solo album by his erstwhile Pink Floyd colleague Syd Barrett. 'All the songs on this album are great,' Waters commented. 'Some of them are GREAT – in capital letters. Syd is a genius.' This was not the first time that Barrett had been awarded the supreme accolade of artistic greatness, nor was it to be the last. Among those who would pay tribute to his unique and surreal approach to musical and lyrical composition were Marc Bolan, David Bowie (who covered Barrett's 'See Emily Play' on his 1973 album *Pin Ups*), Kevin Ayers (who dedicated his 1973 single 'Oh, Wot A Dream' to Syd), the Soft Boys (who, in the early Eighties, recorded affectionate versions of 'Vegetable Man' and 'Astronomy Domine') and, of course, the post-Barrett Floyd themselves. Syd Barrett's status as a cult 'genius', however, is based more on legends of lunacy than on the man's sadly limited musical output.

Born on 6 January 1946, Barrett was a pre-teen music enthusiast, acquiring his first instrument, a banjo, at the age of eleven and his first (acoustic) guitar the

Insets left: Syd Barrett's two solo albums, The Madcap Laughs (top) and Barrett, both released in 1970, helped to fuel the myth of Syd as deranged genius. Above: Barrett on cushion with the early Pink Floyd and (right) with famed mirror-disc Telecaster guitar.

following year. In 1961, he bought an electric one; armed with this and a home-made amplifier he joined Geoff Mott and the Mottoes, short-lived plunderers of the Cliff and the Shadows songbook. After school, he enrolled at technical college, played bass for a spell with Cambridge R&B combo the Hollering Blues and learned Keith Richards' guitar patterns from friend Dave Gilmour. Then, in 1965, he moved down to London to study art; within weeks, the Pink Floyd Sound had begun its evolution.

Strange songs

To begin with, the Sound was confined to extended untamed feedback renditions of 'Louie Louie' and other imported standards. But soon Barrett started to compose, and his gift for the creation of original and eccentric songs was to pave the way for the group's success. A tale of a man obsessed with women's underwear seemed a somewhat unlikely choice for a hit single, but the unorthodox narrative of 'Arnold Layne' was surrounded by seductive musical fare, while the follow-up, 'See Emily Play' – the story of a girl's mental decline – confirmed Barrett's talent for strange yet saleable pop.

Meanwhile, Barrett's guitar-playing

had matured from amateurish splashing to constructive experimentation. What he lacked in technical ability, he compensated for in invention, utilising feedback, echo, slide-work and an immaculately accurate wah-wah technique to inimitable effect. His playing on the startling space-rock epic 'Astronomy Domine', from The Piper At The Gates Of Dawn, set standards of atmospheric intensity that have rarely, if ever, been bettered.

But by the time Piper was released in August 1967, Barrett's mental health was

in a sorry state. Since childhood, his personality had been less than stable, and he had lately been indulging ferociously in LSD. In July, the Floyd had appeared three times on BBC-TV's 'Top Of The Pops' performing 'See Emily Play'. For the first programme, Barrett had worn his best psychedelic pop-star gear; for the second, he had worn the same clothes but appeared not to have removed them since the last time, so stained and crumpled were they. For the third show he had turned up in the scruffiest garb imaginable – baggy old trousers and torn shirt – and, until coaxed, refused to appear.

Home and abroad

On 24 October, Pink Floyd left for their first tour of America – a tour that, thanks to Syd's erratic behaviour, was to be a disaster. At gigs he would stare vacantly into the stage lights and strum one chord throughout the set, oblivious to what the rest of the group were doing. Or he would stand with tongue flopping out and arms hanging motionlessly over the body of his guitar, doing absolutely nothing. The group were invited to mime 'See Emily Play' on 'Dick Clark's Bandstand'; they appeared, but Syd refused to move his lips. They were invited onto the 'Pat Boone Show' for an interview; they appeared, but Syd refused to answer any questions – he just stared through the eyes of the Christian crooner. The American tour was prematurely terminated after eight days.

Back home, Barrett showed that his private muse, at least, had not deserted him. Though never officially released, his 'Vegetable Man', written as a follow-up to the flop single 'Apples And Oranges', was a superb song, combining the most confusing chord and time changes with strange and wryly humorous words: 'There's a kind of stink about blue velvet trousers/In my paisley shirt I look a jerk/And my turquoise waistcoat is quite outta sight/But – oh! – my haircut looks so bad/Vegetable Man where ARE you?' But in public, and with his fellow band members, he showed no signs of improvement. While rehearsing material for a second album, Syd presented a new song called 'Have You Got It Yet?'. This consisted of Syd chanting 'have you got it yet?' above a complex pattern of chords that Waters and Wright found almost impossible to follow. If the other musicians ever got close to 'getting' the sequence, Syd would change it again. They never did get it. In April 1968, by mutual agreement, Barrett and Pink Floyd were divorced.

Barrett spent the rest of the year writing songs for a solo album, which he began recording early in 1969. Released in January 1970, The Madcap Laughs was a collection of charmingly simple songs, sparsely produced (by Gilmour and Waters) and largely unadorned by electric instrumentation – over half the numbers were accompanied only by acoustic guitar. The listener was left to concentrate on the words which were as intriguingly batty as

Above: Syd Barrett on stage with Pink Floyd at Alexandra Palace in 1967. Below: Back on the ground? A shorn Syd in the early Seventies.

ever. Musically, the general feel of the LP was warm and relaxed, suggesting that the singer had, at last, found some stability. However, the follow-up, *Barrett*, released later the same year, gave evidence to the contrary. With backing from drummer Jerry Shirley, Gilmour and Wright, Barrett ran through a collection of songs that ranged from the bubbly commerciality of 'Gigolo Aunt' to the nightmarish stream-of-lunatic-consciousness of 'Rats'.

Following the album's release, Syd returned to Cambridge where he lived in the cellar of his mother's home. He spent his time painting pictures until January 1972, when he made his first public appearance in four years at King's College, where Eddie 'Guitar' Burns was giving a concert. Burns' pick-up backing band consisted of ex-Delivery bassist Jack Monck and Twink, one-time drummer with the Pretty Things, Pink Fairies and Tomorrow. Twink knew Syd from UFO days and, spying him in the audience, invited him on stage to jam.

As a result, Twink and Monck talked Barrett into forming a permanent trio,

Stars. Though under-rehearsed, they made their official debut at Cambridge Corn Exchange in February, alongside Skin Alley and the MC5. Stars were a disaster. Going on last, they started with a slow and out-of-tune version of 'Octopus', from the *Madcap* LP, during which the majority of the audience walked out. Syd seemed bored or bewildered by the occasion; he would stop playing to scratch his nose, he would stop singing for no apparent reason. Then, midway through a song, he quietly put down his guitar and walked from the stage. After Barrett failed to turn up for a second gig, Stars split.

The hand that feeds
Following a further period of seclusion, Barrett was contacted by Peter Jenner and persuaded to come into the studio to record a third album. Before the project was aborted when Syd bit the engineer's hand, he spent the entire session attempting to record an endless, complex and seemingly tuneless guitar instrumental.

Nothing further was heard until the summer of 1975 when Pink Floyd were recording *Wish You Were Here* in Abbey Road studios. One day he turned up and announced, to the astonishment of the group, that he was now ready to play with them again. The Floyd were further astonished by Syd's appearance: he had shaved his head and had put on an incredible amount of weight – the wasted youth of yesteryear had swollen to more than fourteen stone. (Included on *Wish You Were Here* was 'Shine On You Crazy Diamond', a tribute to Syd.)

Since that sad day, Barrett has remained a recluse. But his influence on popular music remained strong, and after a selection of independent label bands recorded a tribute album of his songs EMI released a 'best of the rest' compilation of unreleased material from his album sessions entitled *Opel* (1988).

A great talent Syd Barrett certainly was – a 'genius' possibly. But his tragically befuddled brain never allowed him to prove it.   TOM HIBBERT

Syd Barrett
Recommended Listening

Barrett (Harvest Heritage SHDW 404) (Includes: Terrapin, Octopus, She Took A Long Cold Look, Baby Lemonade, Gigolo Aunt, Effervescing Elephant).

INDEX

v

U.S. HIT SINGLES

1970

JANUARY

3 RAINDROPS KEEP FALLIN' ON MY HEAD
B.J. Thomas

10 RAINDROPS KEEP FALLIN' ON MY HEAD
B.J. Thomas

17 RAINDROPS KEEP FALLIN' ON MY HEAD
B.J. Thomas

24 RAINDROPS KEEP FALLIN' ON MY HEAD
B.J. Thomas

31 I WANT YOU BACK   *Jackson Five*

FEBRUARY

7 VENUS   *Shocking Blue*

14 THANK YOU/EVERYBODY IS A STAR
Sly and the Family Stone

21 THANK/YOU EVERYBODY IS A STAR
Sly and the Family Stone

28 BRIDGE OVER TROUBLED WATER
Simon and Garfunkel

MARCH

7 BRIDGE OVER TROUBLED WATER
Simon and Garfunkel

14 BRIDGE OVER TROUBLED WATER
Simon and Garfunkel

21 BRIDGE OVER TROUBLED WATER
Simon and Garfunkel

28 BRIDGE OVER TROUBLED WATER
Simon and Garfunkel

APRIL

4 BRIDGE OVER TROUBLED WATER
Simon and Garfunkel

11 LET IT BE   *Beatles*

18 LET IT BE   *Beatles*

25 ABC   *Jackson Five*

MAY

2 ABC   *Jackson Five*

9 AMERICAN WOMAN/NO SUGAR TONIGHT
Guess Who

16 AMERICAN WOMAN/NO SUGAR TONIGHT
Guess Who

23 AMERICAN WOMAN/NO SUGAR TONIGHT
Guess Who

30 EVERYTHING IS BEAUTIFUL
Ray Stevens

JUNE

6 EVERYTHING IS BEAUTIFUL
Ray Stevens

13 THE LONG AND WINDING ROAD/FOR YOU
BLUE   *Beatles*

20 THE LONG AND WINDING ROAD/FOR YOU
BLUE   *Beatles*

27 THE LOVE YOU SAVE   *Jackson Five*

JULY

4 THE LOVE YOU SAVE   *Jackson Five*

11 MAMA TOLD ME NOT TO COME
Three Dog Night

18 MAMA TOLD ME NOT TO COME
Three Dog Night

25 (THEY LONG TO BE) CLOSE TO YOU
Carpenters

AUGUST

1 (THEY LONG TO BE) CLOSE TO YOU
Carpenters

8 (THEY LONG TO BE) CLOSE TO YOU
Carpenters

15 (THEY LONG TO BE) CLOSE TO YOU
Carpenters

22 MAKE IT WITH YOU   *Bread*

29 WAR   *Edwin Starr*

SEPTEMBER

5 WAR   *Edwin Star*

12 WAR   *Edwin Star*

19 AIN'T NO MOUNTAIN HIGH ENOUGH
Diana Ross

26 AIN'T NO MOUNTAIN HIGH ENOUGH
Diana Ross

OCTOBER

3 AIN'T NO MOUNTAIN HIGH ENOUGH
Diana Ross

10 CRACKLIN' ROSIE   *Neil Diamond*

17 I'LL BE THERE   *Jackson Five*

24 I'LL BE THERE   *Jackson Five*

31 I'LL BE THERE   *Jackson Five*

NOVEMBER

7 I'LL BE THERE   *Jackson Five*

14 I'LL BE THERE   *Jackson Five*

21 I THINK I LOVE YOU
Partridge Family

28 I THINK I LOVE YOU
Partridge Family

DECEMBER

5 I THINK I LOVE YOU
Partridge Family

12 TEARS OF A CLOWN
Smokey Robinson and the Miracles

19 TEARS OF A CLOWN
Smokey Robinson and the Miracles

26 MY SWEET LORD/ISN'T IT A PITY?
George Harrison

1971

JANUARY

2 MY SWEET LORD/ISN'T IT A PITY?
George Harrison
9 MY SWEET LORD/ISN'T IT A PITY?
George Harrison
16 MY SWEET LORD/ISN'T IT A PITY?
George Harrison
23 KNOCK THREE TIMES *Dawn*
30 KNOCK THREE TIMES *Dawn*

FEBRUARY

6 KNOCK THREE TIMES *Dawn*
13 ONE BAD APPLE *Osmonds*
20 ONE BAD APPLE *Osmonds*
27 ONE BAD APPLE *Osmonds*

MARCH

6 ONE BAD APPLE *Osmonds*
13 ONE BAD APPLE *Osmonds*
20 ME AND BOBBY McGEE *Janis Joplin*
27 ME AND BOBBY McGEE *Janis Joplin*

APRIL

3 JUST MY IMAGINATION *Temptations*
10 JUST MY IMAGINATION *Temptations*
17 JOY TO THE WORLD *Three Dog Night*
24 JOY TO THE WORLD *Three Dog Night*

MAY

1 JOY TO THE WORLD *Three Dog Night*
8 JOY TO THE WORLD *Three Dog Night*
15 JOY TO THE WORLD *Three Dog Night*
22 JOY TO THE WORLD *Three Dog Night*
29 BROWN SUGAR *Rolling Stones*

JUNE

5 BROWN SUGAR *Rolling Stones*
12 WANT ADS *Honey Cone*
19 IT'S TOO LATE *Carole King*
26 IT'S TOO LATE *Carole King*

JULY

3 IT'S TOO LATE *Carole King*
10 IT'S TOO LATE *Carole King*
17 IT'S TOO LATE *Carole King*
24 INDIAN RESERVATION *Raiders*
30 YOU'VE GOT A FRIEND *James Taylor*

AUGUST

7 HOW CAN YOU MEND A BROKEN HEART?
Bee Gees
14 HOW CAN YOU MEND A BROKEN HEART?
Bee Gees
21 HOW CAN YOU MEND A BROKEN HEART?
Bee Gees
28 HOW CAN YOU MEND A BROKEN HEART?
Bee Gees

SEPTEMBER

4 UNCLE ALBERT/ADMIRAL HALSEY
Paul and Linda McCartney
11 GO AWAY LITTLE GIRL *Donny Osmond*
18 GO AWAY LITTLE GIRL *Donny Osmond*
25 GO AWAY LITTLE GIRL *Donny Osmond*

OCTOBER

2 MAGGIE MAY *Rod Stewart*
9 MAGGIE MAY *Rod Stewart*
16 MAGGIE MAY *Rod Stewart*
23 MAGGIE MAY *Rod Stewart*
30 MAGGIE MAY *Rod Stewart*

NOVEMBER

6 GYPSYS, TRAMPS AND THIEVES *Cher*
13 GYPSYS, TRAMPS AND THIEVES *Cher*
20 THEME FROM *SHAFT* *Issac Hayes*
27 THEME FROM *SHAFT* *Issac Hayes*

DECEMBER

4 FAMILY AFFAIR
Sly and the Family Stone
11 FAMILY AFFAIR
Sly and the Family Stone
18 FAMILY AFFAIR
Sly and the Family Stone
25 BRAND NEW KEY
Melanie

U.K. HIT SINGLES

1970

JANUARY

3	TWO LITTLE BOYS	*Rolf Harris*
10	TWO LITTLE BOYS	*Rolf Harris*
17	TWO LITTLE BOYS	*Rolf Harris*
24	TWO LITTLE BOYS	*Rolf Harris*
31	LOVE GROWS	*Edison Lighthouse*

FEBRUARY

7	LOVE GROWS	*Edison Lighthouse*
14	LOVE GROWS	*Edison Lighthouse*
21	LOVE GROWS	*Edison Lighthouse*
28	LOVE GROWS	*Edison Lighthouse*

MARCH

7	WAND'RIN STAR	*Lee Marvin*
14	WAND'RIN STAR	*Lee Marvin*
21	WAND'RIN STAR	*Lee Marvin*
28	BRIDGE OVER TROUBLED WATER	
	Simon and Garfunkel	

APRIL

4	BRIDGE OVER TROUBLED WATER	
	Simon and Garfunkel	
11	BRIDGE OVER TROUBLED WATER	
	Simon and Garfunkel	
18	ALL KINDS OF EVERYTHING	*Dana*
25	ALL KINDS OF EVERYTHING	*Dana*

MAY

2	SPIRIT IN THE SKY	*Norman Greenbaum*
9	SPIRIT IN THE SKY	*Norman Greenbaum*
16	BACK HOME	*England World Cup Squad*
23	BACK HOME	*England World Cup Squad*
30	BACK HOME	*England World Cup Squad*

JUNE

6	YELLOW RIVER	*Christie*
13	IN THE SUMMERTIME	*Mungo Gerry*
20	IN THE SUMMERTIME	*Mungo Gerry*
27	IN THE SUMMERTIME	*Mungo Gerry*

JULY

4	IN THE SUMMERTIME	*Mungo Gerry*
11	IN THE SUMMERTIME	*Mungo Gerry*
18	IN THE SUMMERTIME	*Mungo Gerry*
25	IN THE SUMMERTIME	*Mungo Gerry*

AUGUST

1	THE WONDER OF YOU	*Elvis Presley*
8	THE WONDER OF YOU	*Elvis Presley*
15	THE WONDER OF YOU	*Elvis Presley*
22	THE WONDER OF YOU	*Elvis Presley*
29	THE WONDER OF YOU	*Elvis Presley*

SEPTEMBER

5	THE WONDER OF YOU	*Elvis Presley*
12	TEARS OF A CLOWN	
	Smokey Robinson and the Miracles	
19	BAND OF GOLD	*Freda Payne*
26	BAND OF GOLD	*Freda Payne*

OCTOBER

3	BAND OF GOLD	*Freda Payne*
10	BAND OF GOLD	*Freda Payne*
17	BAND OF GOLD	*Freda Payne*
24	BAND OF GOLD	*Freda Payne*
31	WOODSTOCK	
	Matthew's Southern Comfort	

NOVEMBER

7	WOODSTOCK	
	Matthew's Southern Comfort	
14	WOODSTOCK	
	Matthew's Southern Comfort	
21	VOODOO CHILE	
	Jimi Hendrix Experience	
28	I HEAR YOU KNOCKIN'	*Dave Edmunds*

DECEMBER

5	I HEAR YOU KNOCKIN'	*Dave Edmunds*
12	I HEAR YOU KNOCKIN'	*Dave Edmunds*
19	I HEAR YOU KNOCKIN'	*Dave Edmunds*
26	I HEAR YOU KNOCKIN'	*Dave Edmunds*

1971

JANUARY

2 I HEAR YOU KNOCKIN' *Dave Edmunds*
9 GRANDAD *Clive Dunn*
16 GRANDAD *Clive Dunn*
23 GRANDAD *Clive Dunn*
30 MY SWEET LORD *George Harrison*

FEBRUARY

6 MY SWEET LORD *George Harrison*
13 MY SWEET LORD *George Harrison*
20 MY SWEET LORD *George Harrison*
27 MY SWEET LORD *George Harrison*

MARCH

6 BABY JUMP *Mungo Jerry*
13 BABY JUMP *Mungo Jerry*
20 HOT LOVE *T. Rex*
27 HOT LOVE *T. Rex*

APRIL

3 HOT LOVE *T. Rex*
10 HOT LOVE *T. Rex*
17 HOT LOVE *T. Rex*
24 HOT LOVE *T. Rex*

MAY

1 DOUBLE BARREL
   Dave and Ansil Collins
8 DOUBLE BARREL
   Dave and Ansil Collins
15 KNOCK THREE TIMES *Dawn*
22 KNOCK THREE TIMES *Dawn*
29 KNOCK THREE TIMES *Dawn*

JUNE

5 KNOCK THREE TIMES *Dawn*
12 KNOCK THREE TIMES *Dawn*
19 CHIRPY CHIRPY CHEEP CHEEP
   Middle of the Road
26 CHIRPY CHIRPY CHEEP CHEEP
   Middle of the Road

JULY

3 CHIRPY CHIRPY CHEEP CHEEP
   Middle of the Road
10 CHIRPY CHIRPY CHEEP CHEEP
   Middle of the Road
17 CHIRPY CHIRPY CHEEP CHEEP
   Middle of the Road
24 GET IT ON *T. Rex*
31 GET IT ON *T. Rex*

AUGUST

7 GET IT ON *T. Rex*
14 GET IT ON *T. Rex*
21 I'M STILL WAITING *Diana Ross*
28 I'M STILL WAITING *Diana Ross*

SEPTEMBER

4 I'M STILL WAITING *Diana Ross*
11 I'M STILL WAITING *Diana Ross*
18 HEY GIRL DON'T BOTHER ME *Tams*
25 HEY GIRL DON'T BOTHER ME *Tams*

OCTOBER

2 HEY GIRL DON'T BOTHER ME *Tams*
9 MAGGIE MAY *Rod Stewart*
16 MAGGIE MAY *Rod Stewart*
23 MAGGIE MAY *Rod Stewart*
30 MAGGIE MAY *Rod Stewart*

NOVEMBER

6 MAGGIE MAY *Rod Stewart*
13 COZ I LOVE YOU *Slade*
20 COZ I LOVE YOU *Slade*
27 COZ I LOVE YOU *Slade*

DECEMBER

4 COZ I LOVE YOU *Slade*
11 ERNIE (THE FASTEST MILKMAN IN THE
   WEST) *Benny Hill*
18 ERNIE (THE FASTEST MILKMAN IN THE
   WEST *Benny Hill*
25 ERNIE (THE FASTEST MILKMAN IN THE
   WEST *Benny Hill*